12
Smart Things
to Do When the Booze
and Drugs Are Gone

Choosing Emotional Sobriety through
Self-Awareness and Right Action

ALLEN BERGER, PH.D.

HAZELDEN

Hazelden
Center City, Minnesota 55012
hazelden.org

Library of Congress Cataloging-in-Publication Data

Berger, Allen, 1952–
    12 smart things to do when the booze and drugs are gone : choosing emotional sobriety through self-awareness and right action / Allen Berger.
        p.   cm.
    Includes bibliographical references.
    ISBN 978-1-59285-821-7 (softcover)
    1. Addicts—Rehabilitation.   2. Emotional maturity.   3. Self-help techniques.   I. Title.
    II. Title: Twelve smart things to do when the booze and drugs are gone.
    HV4998.B46 2010
    616.86'03—dc22

                                                                    2010020762

Editor's note
The names, details, and circumstances have been changed to protect the privacy of those mentioned in this publication.

This publication is not intended as a substitute for the advice of health care professionals.

Alcoholics Anonymous, AA, the Big Book, the *Grapevine, AA Grapevine,* and *GV* are registered trademarks of Alcoholics Anonymous World Services, Inc.

Permission to reprint The AA Grapevine, Inc., copyrighted material in this publication does not in any way imply affiliation with or endorsement by either Alcoholics Anonymous or The AA Grapevine, Inc.

14 13 12 11 10   1 2 3 4 5 6

Cover design by David Spohn
Composition by BookMobile Design and Publishing Services

Dedication

I dedicate this book to Tom Sawdei, a kind and gentle friend with a very bright future, who valiantly struggled to see beyond his addiction and society's stigma to the endless possibilities of recovery. I miss you, Tom.

Contents

Foreword

Emotional sobriety has not been given its due recognition in recovery. We have understandably focused all of our energy on the early stages of recovery, but unfortunately we have not sufficiently addressed the many challenges that occur after we "put the plug in the jug." It is my opinion that one of the major causes of relapse is our failure to grow up and address our emotional dependency.

Once in a while, a writer comes along who extends and completes an earlier discovery made about recovery. This is the unique accomplishment of the work of Dr. Allen Berger in explaining the role of emotional maturity in recovery. Dr. Berger expands on Bill Wilson's understanding of emotional sobriety. He bases his work on Bill Wilson's concepts, outlined in his 1958 *AA Grapevine* article titled "The Next Frontier: Emotional Sobriety."

The power of Dr. Berger's book is in his attention to detail. Each chapter is carefully constructed with clear explanations. He provides us with a tool to make a fearless and thorough emotional inventory. He integrates concepts from many different sources in psychology, and he provides us with exceptional case studies that illustrate the working points of the text.

The tasks and instructions set forth in this book provide an excellent guide to emotional sobriety. Dr. Berger defines the problem in easily understood terms as our emotional dependency or our failure to grow up. He explains how our "idealized self" and "false self" create obstacles to our maturation. He then points out the solution as differentiation of the self, and as recovering our lost, true self. He gives us a way of moving beyond emotional dependency in our relationships to a place of autonomy and choice. In a sense, the solution for those who lack emotional sobriety sounds simple: grow up. But of course, if emotional sobriety were that simple, we would all have achieved it long ago. True emotional sobriety is a life's journey, with twists and turns, delays and detours, and much to be learned along the way. Dr. Berger provides a wonderful, detailed road map to guide readers on the journey.

Jerry McDonald, ACATA
Producer, Drug Awareness Hour at the Betty Ford Center

Acknowledgments

Sid Farrar, Hazelden's Editorial and Trade Director, played a crucial role in this book. Sid helped me discover that it was this book that I needed to write next. Sid, I deeply respect your professionalism, insights, honesty, and integrity.

I am also grateful to Sid for assigning Vincent Hyman to this project. Vince was a perfect fit for me. I developed a wonderful collaborative relationship with him. Vince, you were a godsend and helped me tremendously at every stage of this project. The quality and depth of this book are a direct result of your efforts. You served in so many different roles during this process: You were my muse, my critic, my friend, my colleague, and an outstanding editor. Thank you.

I also want to acknowledge the Hazelden marketing staff, especially Lisa Malani and Alison Vandenberg, for their ongoing support and their faith in my work. Our professional relationship means a lot to me.

Tom McCall, my sponsor, plays a crucial role in whatever I do personally and professionally. Tom, for over thirty-eight years, you have been my counsel, my friend, my inspiration, and a safe haven. In fact, in the first year of my recovery, you turned me on to the

Grapevine article that eventually became the inspiration for this book. Thank you, my friend. I will be forever grateful for your love, your support, your wisdom, and your guidance.

And finally I want to acknowledge Southwest Airlines and its wonderful employees. You made my travels safe, comfortable, and enjoyable. Thank you! This entire book was written on Southwest flights between Nashville and Los Angeles.

Introduction
Understanding Emotional Sobriety

This book will help you take the next step in your recovery. It is about the emotional quality of your recovery. It will help you grow up and teach you how to better cope with your emotions. It is about *emotional sobriety.*

The concept of emotional sobriety is not easy to grasp. Let's start with an example.

I want you to meet John. He has been clean and sober for ten years. In the past year, he has been struggling with bouts of anxiety. For a long time he believed he was suffering from an undiagnosed medical problem that was causing his anxiety. First, he thought he was having a heart attack because of irregular heartbeats. After he received a thorough cardiac exam, including a treadmill stress test that showed his heart to be quite healthy, he next thought it might be a brain tumor. But after his MRI was normal, he finally accepted that his anxiety was psychological in nature, not physiological. His sweaty palms, headaches, stomachaches, heart palpitations, slight tremors, and feelings of dread and impending doom were all symptoms of anxiety.

He decided to seek therapy because working the Steps wasn't

giving him enough relief. He needed professional help and so came to see me as a therapist. In the first session, I noted how John seemed to want everything to live up to his expectations. For example, he wanted to start our session by telling me about his past. I was more concerned about what was currently happening in John's life that was giving him trouble. I told him this, and it threw him off balance. It took a considerable amount of time for him to regain his balance. You see, what John expected when he came to therapy was that we were going to delve into his past.

I've learned that in the first five minutes of a therapy session, a client will show you what is wrong and what kind of help they need. John was very rigid. He had many expectations about how things were supposed to be, and when these expectations weren't met, he didn't know what to do. He became upset and lost his emotional balance. As we explored this pattern to his behavior, he began to see how his need to control everything and everyone in his life was the precursor to his anxiety attacks. Once he started to learn how to live more in the here and now, John's anxiety disappeared.

John was sober, but he didn't have *emotional sobriety*. Most of us think of *sobriety* as being free of alcohol and other drugs, and this is true. *Emotional sobriety* is not about being free of emotions—that is impossible. You will always have your emotions. Rather, it's about freeing ourselves from bondage to our emotional states. Emotional sobriety is a state in which we experience our emotions and respect them, but we respond to them the way we would respond to other kinds of information. So, we don't act out in a knee-jerk response to every passing emotional state as if it were our life's rule—or our drug. Nor do we blame our emotional responses on other people. We take full responsibility for our emotions and our choice to act—or not—on the information they feed us.

When you achieve emotional sobriety, you will be able to cope with life on life's terms. You will

- hold on to yourself in relationships, be emotionally balanced, and maintain a healthy perspective on things that are upsetting
- keep the locus of your emotional center of gravity within you and stay grounded during turbulent times
- focus on the things that you can change, and accept and let go of what you can't
- accept your imperfections, and have faith in the "process of recovery"
- know a new level of emotional freedom and peace of mind; you will look at life with a sense of wonderment
- have an illuminated gaze and vision

Very little has been written on this subject. Most of the recovery literature focuses on getting clean and sober and staying clean and sober—and for good reason. We need to put the plug in the jug, and keep it there, before we can work on other issues. Bill Wilson clearly recommended this approach. He said, first the "booze cure" and then on to "the development of much more real maturity and balance" (1958). Breaking the shackles of addiction is necessarily the first step in recovery. But once that obsession and compulsion to drink or use has been lifted, we are faced with *living* clean and sober.

More and more of us are realizing that we haven't truly matured, that our emotional development is arrested. We don't like how we react when things don't go our way. We are aware of the difficulty we have in comforting ourselves and staying balanced when we are disappointed or hurt. We secretly know that we need to grow up emotionally—that there is something wrong with how we react when circumstances or people don't meet our expectations. And because we have developed some degree of insight over the years, we know that our problem is of our own making. But what can we do about it?

Some of us may have trouble accepting this fact. It's hard to admit that we are still immature, especially now that we are clean and sober. But if we are honest with ourselves, it shouldn't be too difficult to see that we are immature. If you have any doubt, just ask a few people who are close to you. Give them permission to give you honest feedback about your reaction when you don't get your way. You might be surprised at what they tell you.

We all have trouble dealing with life on life's terms. I still struggle with this issue, and this past summer I celebrated thirty-eight years of being clean and sober. This is a common problem for all of us who are trying to live clean and sober. That's why this topic is so popular in meetings.

So here's our dilemma: The quality of our recovery is determined by how we respond to the problems or challenges in our lives. But because we don't know how best to respond to these issues, we end up stuck and frustrated. This is at the core of our problem. Over and over again, we expect life to live up to our expectations or specifications. When it doesn't, we try to force the square peg into the round hole. We demand the impossible from ourselves, others, and life itself. And then we get frustrated or angry when things don't go our way. Sometimes we end up feeling depressed or anxious, as well. Many times, these reactions lead to a relapse or a dry drunk.

How do we overcome our emotional handicap—our immaturity—and develop real emotional sobriety? How do we learn how to respond, in a healthier way, to what life expects from us? How do we learn to respond with grace and humility when things don't go our way? Well, that is exactly what this book is about. My goal is to help you become aware of what you are doing that is keeping you immature, and to help you grow up. I want you to become aware of what is interfering with your emotional growth and preventing you from achieving emotional sobriety.

Before we get on our way, I want to introduce you to the psychological concept of differentiation, because it will be quite helpful in understanding emotional sobriety.

Emotional Differentiation

Dr. Murray Bowen, a psychiatrist from Georgetown University, borrowed this concept from developmental cellular biology. I'm not a biologist, so I will present a layman's understanding of this idea.

Cells go through various stages of growth, from less specialized to more specialized. At a very early stage, the cell has the capacity to become many different tissues—an eye cell, or a liver cell, or a muscle cell. At this stage, we call the cell *undifferentiated*. As the cell matures, certain genes get turned "on," or expressed, and others get turned "off," or silenced. As this happens, the cell matures into its destiny as an eye cell or a liver cell or a muscle cell. Here's the really amazing thing: Before a cell has become differentiated, we can move it to another part of the body, and it will assume that part's function. For example, if we relocate an undifferentiated cell whose DNA is programmed to become an eye to the cheek of a fetus, it will become a part of the cheek—it will mature as a cheek cell! The microenvironment surrounding the undifferentiated cell will influence what genes are expressed or silenced in the undifferentiated cell. It will be influenced by the genetic coding of these specialized cells surrounding it, and its basic nature will change accordingly. But if that same cell were *differentiated*, meaning that its genes had expressed themselves, and we relocated it to the cheek, a third eye would grow on the cheek of the fetus. This differentiated cell will not be changed or influenced by the surrounding cells. I guess we can say that this cell has reached maturity.

Dr. Bowen believed that people develop similarly. We begin life *undifferentiated*. If we are encouraged to develop according to our *real-self*, we differentiate. If we continue to unfold in this manner, we will evolve into the person we were meant to be. We will mature accordingly. Our development will be like that of an acorn that grows into a beautiful and deeply unique oak tree. Psychologically, differentiation results in a solid sense of self. The greater our differentiation, the less we will be overly influenced by circumstances or significant others. This doesn't mean that we won't allow ourselves to be influenced. Rather, it means that we have the ability to choose to be influenced, without feeling like we are losing ourselves or that we are being controlled.

If we don't develop along these lines, we will have poor differentiation and a very fragile sense of self. We will feel overly anxious about being loved and accepted. We will become an object in our lives, rather than the subject. As a result, we will be overly concerned with what we have and how others respond to us, rather than focusing on who we are. Our value will therefore be determined by our marketability, and therefore our self-esteem will depend on what we have, our circumstances, and how we are accepted or treated.

The fear that we won't be loved or accepted creates a state of continuous anxiety. We cannot live in this highly anxious state; therefore we must resolve our dilemma. In order to be less anxious, we develop a *false-self*. This false-self is constructed out of our perception of a perfect or idealized-self. The idealized-self is who we think we *should* be, who we have to be, to always be loved and accepted. It is the answer to our search for personal glory and ultimate value.

The idealized-self is different for each of us, because each of us weighs different personal characteristics as important. Some of us will be more concerned with pleasing others, others more concerned with being independent or with having power. The list can go on and on. The point is that our false-self is idiosyncratic; it is unique to our set of personal values.

The more alienated we are from our true-self, the more we identify with who we think we should be. Our lives become tyrannized by "shoulds" and "ought-tos." We are driven to adhere to these rules, regardless of their effect on our lives. Since the fear of being rejected drives this whole operation, the locus of our center of emotional gravity is external. We look toward circumstances or people to make us feel okay.

People who are differentiated, on the other hand, are more self-validated. They hold on to individuality in relationships and do not try to control others, or submit to the control of others, or rebel against or withdraw from others, when pressured. Differentiated people hold on to their sense of self when there is relationship conflict, when they are pressured to submit, or when circumstances don't go as expected. They stay connected to and maintain their sense of self. Or as renowned psychoanalyst Erich Fromm stated, they experience "union with the preservation of integrity" (1956). (As you will see, *union with the preservation of integrity* is a persistent theme when seeking emotional sobriety.)

If we are undifferentiated, we become emotionally fused with others or circumstances, and therefore we are strongly influenced by these things. We respond to emotional fusion in one of three ways: (1) by trying to control people, places, or things, (2) by submitting to the will of others or to the nature of circumstances, or (3) by emotionally withdrawing.

Dr. Bowen believed that differentiation of self existed on a continuum from undifferentiated to differentiated. He saw this continuum as ranging from 0 to 100. Low scores represented undifferentiation, while high scores indicated higher degrees of differentiation. It is important to realize that we pick a partner who is at a similar level of emotional differentiation. If our differentiation is at 70, we will pick someone who is between 65 and 75. Couples or partners who are severely undifferentiated become emotional conjoined twins. They are highly reactive to everything their partner does or says and vice versa.

This also explains why we have more difficulty in a relationship when someone's importance to us increases. If our ability to hold on to our true-self does not keep pace with our partner's increasing level of importance, we will run into trouble. As you will see, we save our worst behavior for those who are most important to us.

Most of us lose ourselves in our lives and in our relationships because of our lack of emotional differentiation. The bottom line is that the more undifferentiated we are, the more difficult it will be to achieve emotional sobriety. In other words, emotional sobriety requires us to have a sense of ourselves and to hold on to ourselves.

To better define emotional sobriety, I want to unpack a letter that Bill Wilson wrote to help a depressed friend. In fact, this was the first piece of literature that mentioned the concept of emotional sobriety. As we review the issues Bill identified in this letter, I will discuss how his insights relate to other ideas in psychology about the development of emotional maturity. Hopefully this will help you understand emotional sobriety.

Bill's Letter on Emotional Sobriety

I think that many oldsters who have put our "booze cure" to severe but successful tests still find that they often lack emotional sobriety. Perhaps they will be the spearhead for the next major development in AA—the development of much more real maturity and balance (which is to say, humility) in our relations with ourselves, with our fellows, and with God.

Those adolescent urges that so many of us have for top approval, perfect security, and perfect romance— urges quite appropriate to age seventeen—prove to be an impossible way of life when we are at age forty-seven or fifty-seven.

Since AA began, I've taken immense wallops in all these areas because of my failure to grow up, emotionally and spiritually. My God, how painful it is to keep demanding the impossible, and how very painful to discover finally, that all along we have had the cart before the horse! Then comes the final agony of seeing how awfully wrong we have been, but still finding ourselves unable to get off the emotional merry-go-round.

How to translate a right mental conviction into a right emotional result, and so into easy, happy and good living— well, that's not only the neurotic's problem, it's the problem of life itself for all of us who have got to the point of real willingness to hew to right principles in all our affairs.

Even then, as we hew away, peace and joy may still elude us. That's the place that so many of us AA oldsters have come to. And it's a hell of a spot, literally. How shall our unconscious—from which so many of our fears, compulsions and phony aspirations still stream—be brought into line with what we actually believe, know and want! How to convince our dumb, raging and hidden "Mr. Hyde" becomes our main task.

I've recently come to believe that this can be achieved. I believe so because I begin to see many benighted ones—

folks like you and me—commencing to get results. Last autumn depression, having no real rational cause at all, almost took me to the cleaners. I began to be scared that I was in for another long chronic spell. Considering the grief I've had with depressions, this wasn't a bright prospect.

I kept asking myself, "Why can't the Twelve Steps help to release depression?" By the hour I stared at the St. Francis prayer . . . "It's better to comfort than to be comforted." Here was the formula, all right. But why didn't it work?

Suddenly I realized what the matter was. My basic flaw had always been dependence—almost absolute dependence—on people or circumstances to supply me with prestige, security, and the like. Failing to get these things according to my perfectionist dreams and specifications, I had fought for them. And when defeat came, so did my depression.

There wasn't a chance of making the outgoing love of St. Francis a workable and joyous way of life until these fatal and almost absolute dependencies were cut away.

Because I had over the years undergone a little spiritual development, the *absolute* quality of these frightful dependencies had never before been so starkly revealed. Reinforced by what Grace I could secure in prayer, I found I had to exert every ounce of will and action to cut off these faulty emotional dependencies upon people, upon AA, indeed, upon any set of circumstances whatever.

Then only could I be free to love as Francis had. Emotional and instinctual satisfactions, I saw, were really the extra dividends of having love, offering love, and expressing a love appropriate to each relation of life.

Plainly I could not avail myself to God's love until

I was able to offer it back to Him by loving others as He would have me. And I couldn't possibly do that if I was victimized by false dependencies.

For my dependency meant demand—a demand for the possession and control of the people and conditions surrounding me.

While those words "absolute dependency" may look like a gimmick, they were the ones that helped to trigger my release into my present degree of stability and quietness of mind, qualities which I am now trying to consolidate by offering love to others regardless of the return to me.

This seems to be the primary healing circuit: an outgoing love of God's creation and His people, by means of which we avail ourselves of His love for us. It is most clear that the real current can't flow until our paralyzing dependencies are broken, and broken at depth. Only then can we possibly have a glimmer of what adult love really is.

Spiritual calculus you say? Not a bit of it. Watch any AA of six months working with a new Twelfth Step case. If the case says, "To the devil with you," the Twelfth Stepper only smiles and turns to another case. He doesn't feel frustrated or rejected. If his next case responds, and in turn starts to give love and attention to another alcoholic, yet gives none back to him, the sponsor is happy about it anyway. He still doesn't feel rejected; instead he rejoices that his one-time prospect is sober and happy. And if his next following case turns out in later time to be his best friend (or romance) then the sponsor is most joyful. But he well knows that his happiness is a by-product—the extra dividend of giving without any demand for return.

The real stabilizing thing for him was having and

offering love to that strange drunk on his doorstep. That was Francis at work, powerful and practical, minus dependency and minus demand.

In the first six months of my own sobriety, I worked with many alcoholics. Not a one responded. Yet this work kept me sober. It wasn't a question of those alcoholics giving me anything. My stability came out of trying to give, not out of demanding that I receive.

Thus I think it can work out with emotional sobriety. If we examine every disturbance we have, great or small, we will find at the root of it some unhealthy dependency and its consequent unhealthy demand. Let us, with God's help, continually surrender these hobbling demands. Then we can be set free to live and love; we may then be able to Twelfth Step ourselves and others into emotional sobriety.

Of course I haven't offered you a really new idea— only a gimmick that has started to unhook several of my own "hexes" at depth. Nowadays my brain no longer races compulsively in either elation, grandiosity or depression. I have been given a quiet place in bright sunshine. (1958)*

Unpacking Bill's Letter
What an incredible document! I believe this letter is one of Bill's most important contributions.

Bill makes an important point about emotional sobriety in the opening comments of his letter. He notes that even though we may have stopped drinking or using, many of us have not achieved emotional sobriety. Emotional sobriety doesn't spontaneously appear.

We have to work hard at growing up. Bill did. In addition to the time he spent working the Steps, getting spiritual direction from the Reverend Sam Shoemaker, spending time alone in contemplation, and working with others, he also sought out psychotherapy. His therapist was the famous Dr. Harry Tiebout, the first psychiatrist to recognize the importance of the fellowship of Alcoholics Anonymous. Bill gained many valuable insights into himself and his feelings as a result of these efforts.

Bill defined emotional sobriety as a "real maturity" and "balance" in our relationship with ourselves, our fellows, and our Higher Power. We cannot have balance if we make what other people think more important than what we think. We cannot have balance or hold on to ourselves if we don't grow up, emotionally. Therefore, it is best to think about emotional sobriety as a by-product of a particular way of being in life.

Bill was an incredibly honest and humble man. He admits that he had major problems in his life because of his "failure to grow up, emotionally and spiritually." Isn't this impressive—the cofounder of AA admitting he was immature? His level of humility and honesty is truly inspiring.

Since maturity is critical for total recovery, our immaturity needs to be addressed in recovery. In several of his writings, Dr. Harry Tiebout identified the cause of emotional immaturity as "infantile aspects of the child's ego that persist into adulthood" (1999). It was Dr. Tiebout who first used the term "king baby" to describe one aspect of our behavior. He observed that we wanted everyone to submit to our will and desires. Yes, you read this correctly; he called us big babies. Recall what I said earlier, that the meaning of life does not come from life living up to our expectations, but rather *how we deal with life's expectations of us*. This attitude is quite impossible to adopt when we are big babies who demand that everyone submit to our will and that we get everything we want, right now.

The foundation for recovery is humility. The Twelve Steps are designed to create and maintain a sense of humility in our lives. We must learn to let go of our selfishness and self-centeredness. We must learn to get out of our own way—or rather, out of the way of our real-self. Therefore humility is also important in achieving emotional sobriety. Humility will ultimately be the foundation upon which we develop the ability to hold on to ourselves; to prevent ourselves from being knocked off balance by people, places, or things; and to not be overly influenced by others. It also puts our needs and desires into proper perspective. Can you begin to see how relevant emotional differentiation is to this entire discussion? In fact, I believe that differentiation is to emotional sobriety as water is to life. Differentiation quenches the thirst of emotional sobriety.

One of the hallmarks of emotional sobriety is honest and humble self-esteem. By self-esteem, I am not talking about the arrogant display of "esteem" for oneself or a pompous assumption of privilege and superiority. *True* self-esteem occurs when we respect our own needs and our desires *as we do those of others*, neither overvaluing nor devaluing them. Until we achieve emotional sobriety, we will either feel less than or better than others. Without emotional sobriety, we will never experience the value of true humility and how it can improve our relationship with ourselves and with others. The first step toward emotional sobriety is to see the effect of our unreasonable expectations.

Bill saw that unreasonable expectations—what he called his "adolescent urges" for "top approval, perfect security, and perfect romance"—created an impossible way of life for him, just as they do for us too. In other words, he realized (1) that he looked outside of himself for validation, wanting "top approval," and (2) that his expectations were both perfectionistic and absolute, wanting "perfect security and perfect romance." These are undeniably twisted expectations.

Looking outside of ourselves for validation is what marital therapist and author Dr. David Schnarch referred to as "other validated self-esteem" (1997). This kind of self-esteem is dependent upon how others react or respond to us. Because this kind of self-esteem is dependent on things that are beyond our control, it is very fragile. When one thing doesn't go our way, or a person doesn't act as we expect them to, down the toilet we go.

Other-validated self-esteem makes us highly reactive. It lowers the threshold of our reactions, because everything that happens to us has implications for our self-esteem. But most of us don't see it this way. We don't want to admit that we are still so self-centered and that we take most things personally. We'd rather think of ourselves as overly sensitive, but the real problem is our self-centeredness and our other-validated self-esteem.

Bill also described how he wanted "perfect security and perfect romance." We are perfectionists. We have very strong and rigid ideas about how life is supposed to be, which is one of the reasons we drank, used other drugs, or did both. We didn't know how to deal with life as it was; we wanted it our way.

Bill also recognized that the emotional issues that were causing him to be depressed were deep within and, for a long time, outside of his consciousness. Bill was very insightful. Sigmund Freud said, "We are being lived by forces within us." What a meaningful observation. This implies that there are forces within us—forces that we are unaware of—that have a very powerful influence on our feelings and behavior. These hidden forces create a huge blind spot.

Bill knew that what lay in his unconscious had to be addressed before he could fully integrate a "right mental conviction" or "right principles" into his life. He knew he had to deal with his "raging and hidden Mr. Hyde." We all have our own Mr. Hyde that we need to come to grips with if we want to achieve emotional sobriety. (More about this in a moment.)

Bill mentioned that his "fears, compulsions and phony aspirations" need to be brought into line with what we know and believe. How do we address these in recovery? The first step is to be honest with ourselves. Our greatest phony aspiration comes from our "perfectionist dreams and specifications." We are perfectionists, whether we care to admit it or not, and we project these feelings onto circumstances and other people. This doesn't mean that we do everything perfectly, because that's impossible. Rather, it means we expect ourselves and others to live up to our perfectionistic specifications. We are absolute, black and white, in our concept of who we think we should be and how life should be. This is a major problem and feeds our emotional dependency. Remember my discussion of the false-self and how we developed it to resolve our anxiety? Well, the solution we adopted became an absolute: This is how *we* must be and how *things* must be. There is no alternative. There is no gray; life is black and white.

There's good news though. Yes, we built a false-self to escape the anxiety of undifferentiation. This false-self seems a prison made of perfectionistic "shoulds." Yet we aren't necessarily left to be imprisoned by our "shoulds" for the remainder of our lives. Emotional freedom is possible. We constructed the false-self, and we can deconstruct it.

Bill tells us there is hope. With much effort, we can grow up. We begin by identifying the problem. Bill identified the culprit behind his unrealistic expectations and depression. His hidden and raging Mr. Hyde was his "almost absolute dependence—on people or circumstances to supply me with prestige, security and the like." His basic problem was "absolute dependence." He was emotionally dependent on people and circumstances and therefore emotionally undifferentiated.

When we are emotionally dependent, how we feel about ourselves is contingent on circumstances and how we are treated by others. The more important a circumstance is to us, the more power it has over our feelings. The more important a person is to us, the more power they have over our feelings. So when we say, "This is making me angry!" or "You are making me angry!" it means we are emotionally dependent. When we are emotionally fused, people or circumstances actually make us feel this way or that. The more emotionally dependent we are, the more influenced we are by circumstances or how others behave or feel.

There's an important concept that I want to introduce at this point. It has to do with how we interact with our environment to get our needs met. Dr. Fritz Perls, a brilliant Gestalt therapist, discussed the difference between "environmental support" and "self support" (1973). When we are emotionally dependent, we rely on environmental support to feel good about ourselves and to meet our needs. When we ask someone how we look, we are manipulating that person for emotional support. We want them to tell us we look good because our self-esteem is dependent upon their impression.

Dr. Perls was highly critical of this behavior: "We are phobic, we avoid suffering, especially the suffering of frustrations. We are spoiled, and we don't want to go through the hell gates of suffering: We stay immature, we go on manipulating the world, rather than to suffer the pains of growing up. This is the story" (1973). Perls is saying that the more mature we are, the more we suffer our frustrations and use that tension to become self-supportive. This means that I stop requiring you to do what I want you to do, in order for me to be okay. I also stop manipulating situations to meet my needs. I stand on my own two feet and support my own feelings or desires. I ask for what I want, rather than manipulate you to say what I want to hear or to do what I want you to do. If you don't want to give me what I want, I grieve or, better yet, appreciate what you do have to offer. But I don't insist upon getting my way.

Dr. Nathaniel Branden, an expert on self-esteem, said, "Self-esteem is the reputation we have with ourselves" (1994). You cannot have true self-esteem unless you stop manipulating others to make you feel okay. You cannot have emotional sobriety until you deal with your emotional dependency.

Bill realized that there was a connection between his emotional dependency and his depression. For Bill, depression always followed not being able to get others to submit to his will (environmental support). He realized that he became depressed when he failed to get people or circumstances to meet his perfectionistic dreams and specifications. When life didn't meet his expectations, he got depressed. He took it personally.

This is another characteristic of emotional dependency, which we call *emotional fusion*. Bill was emotionally fused with people and circumstances: His sense of himself was determined by what he saw reflected in how life conformed to his expectations. If things went his way, he was fine; if they didn't, he became angry and then depressed. In order to grow up, Bill came to the conclusion that he needed to use "every ounce of will and action to cut off these faulty emotional dependencies upon people, upon AA, indeed, upon any set of circumstances whatever."

Yes, you read the last paragraph correctly. Bill said that he had to end all his dependencies, even his dependency upon AA. Quite a remarkable statement coming from the cofounder of the AA program. This underscores a very important point: A Twelve Step program does not replace our dependency on drugs with a dependency on the program. Rather it helps us become free of all dependencies: first our dependency on alcohol or other drugs, and then our dependency "upon people, upon AA, indeed upon any set of circumstances whatever." *This is the true essence of emotional sobriety.*

Please note that Bill mentioned that he had to "exert every ounce of will and action to cut off these faulty emotional dependencies." This point is often misunderstood in recovery. Willpower has a very bad reputation in recovery. Our defiant reliance upon willpower locked us into a vicious cycle with our addiction. While willpower interferes with surrendering to the First Step, it becomes essential to recovery beyond the First Step because without your willingness, nothing will change. Bill stepped up to take action against his dependencies. He made his desire to change intentional. Taking right action and total responsibility for one's feelings and actions is characteristic of people with high self-esteem. Self-esteem and emotional sobriety walk hand in hand.

Bill also mentioned the lesson he learned in working with others. Early on in his recovery, he worked with several people who did not get sober. Here we are introduced to a very important principle of emotional sobriety: *intrinsic motivation.* Emotional sobriety is based on doing the right thing for the sake of our own integrity. If this is our true motivation, then we do not require the other person to respond in a particular manner. There is no expectation attached to our behavior. They are free to respond as they wish. I am I, and you are you. Bill's work with people who did not get sober might be considered work done out of intrinsic motivation. The work was done because it was the right thing to do, not because it would bring fame. It was done regardless of whether the person would sober up or not. Bill was Bill, and the other was the other.

Emotional dependency interfered with Bill's ability to love and to be loved. It created what Erich Fromm called an "immature love" (1956). The essence of this kind of love is, "I love you because I need you." When we are emotionally dependent, we become like emotional conjoined twins. We lose our individuality, our sense of self, in our connection with our partner.

It is easy to see how this kind of love becomes driven by demands. People, and the conditions surrounding us, must submit to our will and desires, or else. We demand complete and blind obedience. And if challenged, we employ whatever tactics necessary to manipulate the challenger into submitting to our will.

We need to grow up and get over our emotional dependency before we can understand what Bill called "adult love." Erich Fromm called it "mature love" (1956). As noted earlier, mature love is based on a "union with the preservation of integrity." When we stand on our own two feet, we can join, without losing our individuality. Love becomes based on personal choice and desire, rather than dependency. Adult love says, "I want you because I love you."

Bill gives us the key that can unlock much wisdom and maturity in our lives. He points out that whenever we are disturbed, regardless of the magnitude of the issue, our reaction occurs because we have "some unhealthy dependency and its consequent unhealthy demand." Really take a moment and let this sink in. It will blow your mind to realize that whenever you are upset, it means that your raging and hidden Mr. Hyde is the culprit.

The Path to Emotional Sobriety

Emotional sobriety sounds great, doesn't it? It's like warm apple pie with homemade vanilla ice cream—who wouldn't want it? But how do we achieve this state of being? How do we unhook our emotional dependency and learn to stand on our own two feet?

Well, that is what the remainder of this book is all about. I have selected twelve smart things you can do to grow up and unhook your emotional dependency. I refer to them as "smart things" because these are things done by people who have a high degree of emotional intelligence, self-esteem, and emotional resilience. Here are the twelve smart things:

1. Know yourself—and how to stay centered.
2. Stop allowing others to edit your reality.
3. Stop taking things personally.
4. Own your projections as an act of integrity.
5. Confront yourself for the sake of your integrity.
6. Stop pressuring others to change, and instead pressure yourself to change.
7. Develop a healthy perspective toward yourself, your feelings, and your emotional themes.
8. Appreciate what is.
9. Comfort yourself when you are hurt or disappointed.
10. Use your personal compass to guide your life.
11. Embrace relationship tensions as the fuel for personal growth.
12. The "problem" is not the real problem.

After reading this list, I immediately thought of the line from the Big Book, "What an order, I can't go through with it!" Please don't expect yourself to master each and every one of these suggestions. As long as you are willing to experiment with these, you will take a big step in your emotional development. Some will be more relevant for you than others. You pick and choose the best to focus on.

My hope is that by the time you finish reading this book, you will have learned how to maintain your emotional balance within yourself and in relation to others.

Smart Thing 1
Know Yourself— and How to Stay Centered

Those of us who have been trudging the road of recovery understand the importance of inward searching. At some point, we realized that if we were going to stay clean and sober, we had to stop blaming others for what was wrong with our lives, let go of our self-righteousness, stop our futile self-justifications, and make amends to those we hurt. Finally, we dared to become honest with ourselves and faced the painful truth that our problems were of our own making. Bill Wilson put it this way, "We must awake or we die" (1957).

If we have been rigorous in our efforts, we have made a "painstaking and vigorous effort" to uncover and discover our emotional liabilities. While this task is straightforward and simple, it is not easy. Our false-self cries out against these efforts. We are thwarted by our blind spots and delusions at every turn. Do not be disheartened, this kind of resistance is expected. It took us many years to construct our false-self, and dismantling it will take persistent effort. Hang in there!

An interesting phenomenon occurs for some of us in the first ten years of recovery. We started the journey of recovery with a sense of urgency. We were told that we needed to accept the nature of our fatal malady and give up on the idea that we could control our drinking or using. We learned as much as we could about our illness and set out on the difficult course of taking a personal inventory and cleaning house. We desperately wanted to be clean and sober and to find true peace of mind. In the early years of recovery, our self-discovery revolved around understanding our emotional deformities and how they related to our disease. We wanted relief from our mental obsession with alcohol or other drugs, and absolution for the wreckage of our past. But once our compulsion to drink or use was lifted and we started enjoying some degree of peace of mind, many of us slacked off on our efforts. We gradually decreased our meeting attendance—maybe going just enough to keep ourselves sober, but not enough to stay in touch with real recovery. We became complacent. Our efforts, at working the Steps or in working with others, became more sporadic. We mistakenly treated recovery like it was an event, rather than a process.

Many of us felt our obsession and compulsion to drink or use lift, but we were still not enjoying the full emotional benefits of recovery. Some of us were even accused of being on a "dry drunk." Oftentimes, those who are closest to us sensed something was wrong before we became aware of it.

Then trouble really hit. We began to experience feelings we didn't know how to handle. We either ended up compromising our integrity in some way, or we developed a severe depression or a crippling anxiety. We ended up in crisis. A crisis of personal limitation. A crisis that was created because we stopped growing in our recovery. We stopped working on our recovery. We forgot that recovery is like walking up an escalator that is going down. When we quit climbing, we regressed.

Do not be alarmed if this has happened or is happening to you.

The crisis you are facing doesn't mean that something is wrong with you. Quite the contrary. It means that something deep within is right. Within us is an evolutional urge to grow, to strive toward wholeness or self-actualization. When we ignore this basic need, we become spiritually sick. Because this basic need won't be denied, we unconsciously create a crisis to provide ourselves with the opportunity to grow up, to take the next step in our emotional and spiritual development, to wake up.

If you have come to this crossroad in your recovery, you have to make a choice. You can either continue on your dry drunk—which may ultimately lead to full-blown relapse—or start climbing up that escalator again. You can either keep doing what you have been doing or renew your effort at self-discovery and take your recovery up to a whole new level, just as Bill Wilson did. The choice is yours, but if you choose to ignore what is going on, I hope you will at least be honest with yourself about the choice you are making to ignore an opportunity for growth and to develop real emotional sobriety.

Of course, you don't have to manufacture a crisis to focus on the emotional quality of your recovery—just like people no longer need to hit bottom to begin recovery. You can raise your consciousness and take on this challenge by accepting the importance of this emotional aspect of your recovery.

If you choose to step up and seek emotional sobriety, then it is important to take an *emotional inventory*. The purpose of making a searching and fearless emotional inventory is quite familiar to those of us who have worked the Twelve Steps. It is to "find exactly how, when, and where our natural desires have warped us" (AA 1981, 43). This means we need to reach beyond those things that are superficially wrong with us, like our anger, our fear of rejection, our indecisiveness, our ambivalence, or our jealousy. These emotions are symptoms—they are the smoke, not the fire, of our lack of emotional sobriety. We need to identify the patterns in our life and their emotional theme in order to damp the fire that generates the smoke.

Bill Wilson demonstrated the importance of taking an emotional inventory. The content of his letter in the introduction was based on what he discovered when he searched deep within himself to understand the underlying cause of his depression. He identified the nature of the emotional pattern connected with his depression. Bill realized that his unreasonable expectations for people and circumstances to meet his "perfectionist specifications and dreams" were created by an "almost absolute dependence on people and circumstances." I believe that if we are honest with ourselves, we will identify with Bill. We will see this pattern in our lives too.

There's a paradox that operates here. We cannot change by trying to be what we are not, by trying to appear more together and mature than we actually are. The heart of emotional sobriety comes from grappling with the difference between our false-self—the one we have constructed to make ourselves more loved—and our true-self.

Let's revisit the concept of false-self and true-self, discussed first in the introduction. Have you ever seen a beautiful bonsai tree? A bonsai artist works patiently over many years to constrain what should be a full-sized tree into perfect miniature. The artist constantly prunes the tree, wraps wires around its branches to shape them, deprives it of water, and trims its roots to fit a tiny pot. Such a tree becomes perfect to look at. And yet . . . and yet. It is not its true-self. It is a tree made to conform to a *vision* of miniature perfection.

Every one of us was anxious or hurt in some form—whether real or perceived—as a child, and we developed an image of how we *should* be in order for the world to love us—a set of rules that, if followed, would make us "perfect." If we are honest, we will see that our rules have made bonsai of us—bonsai of the soul. We are so afraid that our true-self is unlovable that we coil our soul with wire, drink just enough water to stay alive but never enough to quench, and trim our roots. Like the bonsai artist, we spend years warping our true-self into a false-self. A few of us are masters at this and we seem, to others, to be perfect. But the reality is that we have constrained our true-self in an attempt to be loved. This is the impact of our perfectionist specifications—to warp our true selves to fit the rules we think will make us lovable. The bonsai'd soul is the false-self.

No human can live in such self-made bondage without breaking out now and then. And when we do, we act out in frightening ways—often in ways that betray the perfect false-self we've worked so hard to create.

In emotional recovery, we learn to remove the coils, to drink enough water, to plant our souls in earth that is rich and large enough to nurture us and mature us. And we learn to accept that some of our branches will be beautiful, and some will be scarred, and some will be laughable. We learn that as we learn to accept our true-self. This is the process of self-differentiation.

Bill's honest, inward searching helped him mature. It helped him shed his unrealistic expectations of others (and of himself)—it helped him shed the coils he'd wrapped around his world. His search helped him discover the true-self within. And this is the truth Bill uncovered: *Change begins when we admit and face who we are.* Bill admitted that he hadn't grown up and that he was emotionally dependent. Honesty set him free, but only because he had the courage to live it. Honesty will set you free too.

Guidelines for an Emotional Inventory

Bill provided us with a powerful format for identifying the emotional pattern in our lives. He stated, "If we examine every disturbance we have, great or small, we will find at the root of it some unhealthy dependency and its consequent unhealthy demand."

If you are ready to take an emotional inventory, then follow these simple instructions. For the next couple of days, keep a log of everything that bothers you. I have designed a form for this purpose. There is a user-friendly version on page 173. Make copies before you begin the emotional inventory.

The Emotional Sobriety Inventory Form

Upsetting event	Unhealthy dependency	Unreasonable expectation, claim, or demand	Your reaction, or how you responded to the situation	In order to stay centered, I need to realize that _____.

As you can see, the first column of the Emotional Sobriety Inventory Form is where you will record any event or thing that bothered you, disturbed you, or upset you. The magnitude of how upset you felt is irrelevant. Describe the event regardless of whether you were upset a lot or a little. For example, if you were driving to the grocery store and someone cut you off and you got mad, describe this event in the first column. If you came home from work and your partner failed to greet you with a kiss or a hello, and you felt upset, write it down. If you were at an AA meeting and you raised your hand to share, but you weren't selected by the leader and you got upset, describe what happened in the first column. If you did a great job on an assignment at work and you weren't recognized for your efforts and you felt hurt, write this down. If your child embarrassed you during a play date because she wouldn't share one of her toys with the other child, write it down. Anything and everything, big or little, that bothers you over the next couple of days is to be logged in the first column. When you have recorded these events for at least two days, you have completed the first part of the emotional inventory.

The next step is to put aside a block of time, at least an hour, and pull out the emotional inventory form again. You are going to focus on completing the second column. As you can see, the second column asks you to identify the *unhealthy dependency* that was underlying your emotional reaction. For example, if you were cut off on your way to the grocery store, the unhealthy dependency might be, "My welfare and safety depends on how other people drive." If you weren't recognized by your supervisor for your great work, then the unhealthy dependency might be something like, "I depend on my supervisor to make me feel good about my efforts and accomplishments at work." If your child embarrassed you during a play date, your unhealthy dependency might be, "My self-esteem depends on how my child behaves."

This work might be difficult because you aren't going to like seeing how emotionally dependent you are on people or circumstances. If you get stuck, ask for help from a close friend, your spouse, your sponsor, or your therapist. If you need to motivate yourself, then remind yourself that in order to grow up, you need to face your dependencies.

When you have completed the second column, you are ready to move on to the next column. In this column, you will identify the unreasonable expectation, claim, or demand created by your emotional dependency. For example, if you are focusing on your reaction when you were cut off, the unreasonable expectation might be "I expect people to pay attention to me when they are driving." If you weren't recognized at work for your effort, then your demand might be something like, "I demand that my supervisor always recognize me and my efforts." If your child embarrassed you during a play date, your unreasonable expectation might be, "I expect my child to always behave the way I want her to."

(Do this emotional inventory enough, and you may even develop a sense of humor about it, laughing at yourself while you are writing down your demands and expectations. It's truly comical how absurd, unreasonable, and self-centered we can be.)

In column four, you will describe how you reacted to the situation. Your reaction will fall into one of three categories:

1. *Moving against* people or trying to control them
2. *Moving toward* people by submitting to their will or trying to please them
3. *Moving away* from people by withdrawing or emotionally stonewalling them

We are all capable of doing any one of these three things, but typically we have a dominant reaction. Bill Wilson moved against people. This was how he dealt with his emotional dependency. He tried to control people and circumstances to get them to meet his specifications.

Let's say you were disappointed that your spouse did not greet you when you came home. You felt hurt and then you went up to your bedroom and closed the door. Your reaction would be described as *moving away* or *emotionally withdrawing*. If you verbally attacked your partner, saying what a lousy and selfish person they were, then your reaction would be classified as *moving against* people. If you swallowed your hurt and made an excuse for them, like they must have had a bad day, then your reaction is *moving toward* people.

If you are rigorously honest with yourself during this process, you will be able to see the degree to which your emotional dependency is affecting your life. You will also see how you typically cope with your emotional dependency by either moving against people, moving toward people, or moving away from people.

If you are honest with yourself, you will also see the nature of your "perfectionist specifications." I call these our *rules*. We all have a set of rules about how we are supposed to behave or feel, how others are supposed to act, and how life is supposed to be. Just as coils of wire constrict and shape the growth of the bonsai tree, our rules are coils we wrap around our emotions, our relationships, and our expectations of life. Because of our emotional dependency, we demand life to conform to our rules and expectations. This sets us up for many disappointments, conflicts, and problems.

If the bonsai artist removes the coils from the branches of the miniature tree, stops constricting its roots, and transplants it to a better place, the tree will begin to grow. It will spread its roots, its branches will reach out, and it will grow into its natural form. Until we remove our rules—our emotional dependency on others and circumstances—we will not be able to stand on our own two feet and grow up.

Bill wrote in his letter, "How shall our unconscious—from which so many of our fears, compulsions and phony aspirations still stream—be brought into line with what we actually believe, know and want! How to convince our dumb, raging and hidden 'Mr. Hyde' becomes our main task." Sometimes the constraints of our rules overcome us, and we act in crazy ways. When the absurdity or damage of our perfectionistic rules is obvious even to us (other people will have seen it long ago), we come face-to-face with our own Mr. Hyde. But there is a fearful wrenching that comes from letting him go. We fear that we will be left with nothing, because for many years we have identified ourselves with our false-self, the self that spawned our Mr. Hyde. Dr. James Bugental, a brilliant psychotherapist, noted that the nakedness that comes from letting go of these old patterns "seems so, and is so, terribly vulnerable and truly mortal" (1978). But it is only through relinquishing our dependencies and our false-self that we can set forth naked and direct into a healthier relationship with ourselves and others, and so into emotional sobriety.

We cannot have a breakout experience without releasing ourselves from Mr. Hyde's control. Remember the wisdom of the Big Book: "Some of us have tried to hold on to our old ideas and the result was nil until we let go absolutely" (AA 2001, 58). This idea was critical early in our recovery, but is highly relevant to this stage of our recovery as well.

This chapter has been about getting to know yourself as you truly are—warts and all. Now that we have seen how ridiculous and unreasonable we can be, what can we do about it? The answer lies in learning how to hold on to ourselves, in learning how to be self-supportive and to keep our emotional center of gravity within. The solution begins with gaining a new perspective about ourselves and our expectations.

Gaining new perspective is what the fifth column in the inventory table is about—it is where we discover what we need to do to stay centered. But I don't want you to worry about that just yet. You will return to this task later, once you have read the rest of this book. By then you will have a better idea of how to hold on to yourself and unhook your emotional dependency.

In the next chapter, you will learn that unhooking your emotional dependency begins by not letting other people edit your reality.

Smart Thing 2

Stop Allowing Others to Edit Your Reality

In the previous chapter, you conducted an emotional inventory and identified the ways that emotional dependency is affecting your life. Did you list any situations where you were feeling one way about something, and then someone else influenced your feelings about the event? If not, I believe that if you extended the length of time of the log, you would have eventually described this kind of situation.

Remember, emotional sobriety helps you know yourself, know where your center is, and hold on to it. One of the things you need to learn to do to hold on to your center is to stop letting other people *edit your reality*. Our emotional dependency pulls for a certain kind of togetherness or connection. It demands that we feel the same, and think the same, if we are to feel close to another person. So if we feel a certain way about something, we demand that our partner or friends feel this way too. If not, we falsely conclude that we aren't together. Remember, this kind of closeness is emotional fusion, not genuine intimacy.

If you are rigorously honest with yourself, you know that you have a long way to go. Do not be discouraged; no one among us is perfect. The point is to be willing to grow, to learn, to face your emotional dependency, take right action, accept yourself, and strive to become your best possible self.

Bill Wilson realized that to find a healthy balance in his life, he needed to cut away his faulty dependencies, to fully unhook these hexes. We achieve this by learning to hold on to our *self*. Let's spend a moment talking about this concept.

Holding on to our *self* involves staying centered. We stay centered by balancing our desire to please, connect, and join with our desire to follow our own directives, to be ourselves. These two basic needs—togetherness and individuality—are constantly operating in our lives. They are like gravitational forces that continuously influence our behavior. When we hold on to our center, we honor both of these needs equally. We connect with our partner or friends and allow them to influence us without threatening our individuality. We make a *choice* to be influenced. We honor our individuality at the same time we honor our desire for togetherness. As I noted when explaining the concept of emotional sobriety, Erich Fromm called this "union with the preservation of integrity" (1956).

Do not be dismayed if you are struggling with this. Few of us have achieved this level of maturity. There is hope, however. It is possible to stay centered in this way, but doing so is going to take effort. Bill realized this. He knew he had to exert every ounce of willpower to accomplish this task. You, too, will need to make this kind of commitment if you want emotional sobriety.

As with anything we are asked to do in recovery, our effort is tangible evidence of our level of commitment to recovery. So the degree of your effort corresponds to your investment in recovery. As I discussed in my last book, *12 Stupid Things That Mess Up Recovery*, you need to commit at least as much effort, if not more, to your recovery as you invested in your drinking or using. *Half-measures avail us nothing!* You will need to go to great lengths to achieve emotional sobriety.

Remember, when our demands for togetherness are not met, we typically respond by either moving against the person, moving toward them, or moving away from them. But instead of solving the problem, these emotional reactions make it worse. They are like running up to a fire and throwing a bucket of gasoline at it, hoping to douse the flames.

So what is the solution? You need to learn how to stay connected while keeping hold of your individuality. This sounds simple, but it's not easy to do. Let's see how this principle applies to not letting other people edit our reality.

Here's a situation a couple described during a therapy session. Mary said she had a terrible weekend. On Saturday afternoon, her son, Jacob, got his first base hit during a Little League game. She told me that she was beside herself with joy and pride. From what she described, you would have thought that her son had just won the World Series.

On the other hand, Juan, her husband, wasn't as excited. He was very measured in his response. Yes, it was great that Jacob got a base hit, but it wasn't something to go crazy over and cheer about. "It was only a base hit. What's the big deal?" he exclaimed.

Mary was devastated. Juan had rained on her parade. "How dare he?" she thought.

Whenever Mary got hurt, she moved against people. So she went after Juan at the baseball field. She set out on a vicious assault of Juan's character: "What an ass you are! You can't even allow me to be excited without putting me down. What do you think that does to our son? He probably feels real bad that his father isn't proud of him." She concluded her diatribe with, "You are a real jerk!"

Juan just shook his head and whispered underneath his breath,

"What a bitch!" He didn't say anything else because he didn't want the situation to get worse. So he just walked away. He didn't talk to Mary for the rest of the weekend. Does any of this sound familiar? Using the language we learned earlier, Mary *moved against* Juan when he didn't feel the same way she did.

Here's another story about a common dilemma. Alonzo celebrated six months of recovery by getting a six-month chip at his home group. It had been a tough six months, but he made it, one day at a time. This time he knew it was really different. He was reaching out for fellowship by getting to meetings early and staying late, he got a sponsor and called him daily, and he was working the Steps.

This was, however, Alonzo's third attempt at getting clean and sober. His wife, Inca, was fed up. She was bitter and angry, and close to filing for a divorce. She wanted off the emotional merry-go-round that she ended up on when Alonzo was drinking and using. "Enough is enough," she told herself. She was skeptical of Alonzo's efforts. She had been through this twice before. Alonzo told her the same thing each time. "I swear, this time it will be different." But it never was. He relapsed both times. She didn't trust him, not one bit.

So when Alonzo came home from the meeting proudly displaying his six-month chip, Inca was subdued. She stated in an obligatory tone, "That's great."

Alonzo sensed that her heart wasn't in it. He instantly felt disappointed and withdrew. He didn't say a word to her for the next couple of days. He was very hurt and had thoughts like "She'd rather see me drunk again" and "She doesn't really support my recovery." He started to wonder why he even bothered. Alonzo *moved away* from Inca when she did not share his pride and enthusiasm.

Now meet Joan and Ken. They were a very attractive, stylish, and hip couple. They could have easily posed for the cover of *GQ* magazine. Ken was a CEO of a new company and Joan was a talent agent in Hollywood. They were very popular and had a full social calendar. Joan had beautiful, long blond hair that was down past her waist. She wanted to surprise Ken and change her hairstyle. She decided to go real short—pixie short. She was tired of all the work her long hair required and wanted a style easier to care for and cooler for the summer. Her hairstylist did a great job, and she loved her new look. Unfortunately, when Ken saw her, he didn't like it. In fact, he was furious that she would do something so drastic without talking to him about it first. He felt betrayed. It was almost as if Joan had had an affair rather than a new hairstyle. Joan's response was to feel depressed and very threatened. She apologized profusely to Ken and begged for his forgiveness. She wasn't able to feel okay unless he forgave her. Needless to say, she had a difficult week until the day that Ken finally said that he would forgive her, but only if she agreed never to do something like this again without first asking him. Joan swore her allegiance to Ken's demands. Joan *moved toward* Ken when he did not feel the same excitement she did about her new style.

The greater the interdependence of functioning in a relationship, the more likely people are to feel threatened by one another. In each of the examples above, at least one party in the couple was deeply threatened when the other party did not share the same feeling. But emotional dependence isn't just about how couples relate to each other. Allowing people to edit our reality happens in other kinds of relationships as well. I recall talking to a very bright young scientist, Juanita. She wanted to be a medical doctor. Her father was a radiologist, and she was very motivated to follow in his steps. She was an above-average student in high school, but because of an emotional problem, her grades did not reflect her true academic ability. In her junior year of high school she spoke with an academic advisor. Juanita told him about her desire to go to medical school. His reaction stopped Juanita from pursuing her dream. She remembered it as if it happened yesterday. He said, "You will never get into medical school. You should try something else." She was devastated. She swallowed his conclusion whole and gave up her dream. What a pity. I am certain she would have made an outstanding doctor.

These were four different situations, but they all had the same theme in common. Mary, Alonzo, Joan, and Juanita all let others edit their reality. Mary was extremely excited about her son's base hit. Alonzo was proud that he received a six-month chip. Joan liked her new haircut. Juanita wanted to go to medical school. But because of their emotional dependency, they let the gravitational pull of "togetherness" move them off their center of gravity.

Each of them responded to their emotional dependency differently. Mary moved against her husband and attacked him. Alonzo moved away from Inca and withdrew from her. Joan moved toward Ken and asked for forgiveness; she submitted to his control. Juanita swallowed whole the counselor's conclusion that she couldn't get in to medical school and surrendered her dream. Juanita's choice was a form of moving toward—of seeking acceptance by agreeing with another's perception.

As mentioned earlier, the only way to be self-supportive is to maintain your boundary, your autonomy, as you stay connected. Here's what that would look like in each of these situations.

Let's start with Mary. Mary would of course initially feel the tug of her emotional dependency when her husband described his different reaction to their son's hit. Instead of automatically reacting to this tug, she would remind herself that it is okay to have different feelings about the event. She would tell herself that her husband's difference with her is not a reflection of his lack of love for her or their son. It doesn't mean that they are not close. It simply means that he feels differently about it. Mary would accept their difference and continue to enjoy her excitement.

Alonzo would feel hurt by Inca's blasé response to his six-month sobriety celebration, but then he'd step back and remind himself that he is working on his recovery for his own sake. Though it would be nice if Inca could be more supportive and have more faith in him, Alonzo would see that Inca has good reason to feel differently. She is on her own journey. Her reaction doesn't subtract anything from what Alonzo has been doing. In fact, when Alonzo thinks about it, there's a benefit to Inca's reaction. It reminds him to work on his recovery for the right reason—because he needs to address this problem in his life, rather than to gain Inca's love or approval.

Here's what an emotionally sober Joan would do. She would acknowledge that she felt disappointed that Ken didn't like her new hairstyle. She would even seriously consider agreeing with Ken's request to let him know when she was going to make such a drastic change or decision in the future. But if Joan liked her hair the way it was cut, then it was unfortunate that Ken didn't. His reaction wouldn't erase how Joan felt about her hair. She might even be able to say something to Ken like, "Hon, I know that you love me, not just my hair, and after your disappointment is over I am certain you will remember this and realize what is really important between us."

Here's what Juanita would have done if she were more differentiated. No question about it, she would have been taken aback at the advisor's recommendation. But she would have held on to her dream. She might have persisted and asked the counselor to tell her what she needed to do to get in to medical school given her grades. She wouldn't have given up. She would have continued to research the question to find some way that she could overcome her high school grades to get in to medical school.

Did you notice a pattern to the practice of not letting other people edit your reality? There's really a four-step process at work in each case:

1. The *first step* in this process is to become aware of and acknowledge your feelings, your hurt, your disappointment, and especially the anxiety related to feeling that your togetherness is threatened.
2. The *second step* is to reflect on the cause of the feeling until you understand its source.
3. The *third step* is to reflect on what you really want in a nonanxious, calm fashion.
4. And finally, if appropriate, the *fourth step* is to respond to the event that triggered the feeling in a way that both affirms your personal boundaries and yet deals with the triggering event respectfully and responsibly.

This is not always easy. The first step can be very difficult for anyone, especially those of us in recovery who have long medicated our feelings like anxiety with chemicals. We may have trouble getting in touch with what we are feeling. Here's a way to become more aware of what you are feeling. Focus your awareness on any subtle nonverbal or cognitive signs. These may be an indicator that something more is going on within us than we consciously experience. Maybe we feel a slight twinge in our gut. We might let out a huge sigh. Our heart rate might increase. We might start daydreaming or feeling confused. Our hands may become cold and clammy. We might feel light-headed. Our throat may constrict. We might start shaking our foot or tapping our fingers. These behaviors might be communicating something to us about what we are feeling. *How are we going to know?*

I have a suggestion. I am certain it is going to feel a bit strange if you try it, but you might find it useful. Complete the following sentence:

"If my foot could talk, it would say _____
(fill in the blank)."

Or,

"If the twinge in my stomach could talk, it would
say _____ (fill in the blank)." Modify this
incomplete sentence to fit your situation and see what
you discover.

Once you have identified the feeling, step back and reflect on what triggered your reaction. Mary would realize that she reacted when she felt threatened because her husband felt differently than she. Alonzo would realize that he became disappointed and withdrawn because Inca didn't validate his efforts and his accomplishment. Joan would see that she felt threatened because her husband didn't like her independent action or her choice of a hairstyle. Juanita would realize that she was devastated because she wanted the advisor's approval and emotional support to pursue her goal.

Once you have identified the feeling, you need to step back and soothe yourself. It's important to reflect on what you want from a nonanxious posture. You need to do whatever you can to calm yourself down. Take a walk, go exercise at the gym, say the Serenity Prayer, call a friend or your sponsor. Once you are more relaxed, then think about *what you really want*. Remember, you are striving to achieve a balance between togetherness and individuality. Try not to fall out of one side of the bed or the other. For instance, after Mary calms down, she might realize that she wants a relationship in which both she and her partner can freely declare and share their thoughts and feelings. Alonzo might gain the perspective that if you want to be understood, you need to be understanding. Joan might see that her husband does care about her, which is why he reacted so strongly. Juanita might step back and reclaim her dreams. They are of course her dreams, not the advisor's.

Once you have gained perspective, see if there is anything you need to say to set your boundaries and communicate what you want. To do this effectively, you need to deliver the entire message. For instance, Mary might say to her husband, "Juan, I was initially disappointed that you didn't feel like I felt about our son's hit. Instead of attacking you like I usually do, I stepped back and realized that I felt our togetherness was threatened. Sometimes I still have this absurd idea that we need to feel and think the same way for us to be close. I want to be close to you all the time, but I also want there to be room for our individuality."

Alonzo might say to Inca, "I was initially disappointed that you did not validate my efforts. As I thought about it, I realized that you still don't trust me, and for good reason. I've made many false promises in the past. I'll keep doing what I need to do, and hopefully one day I will earn your trust."

Again, the goal is to acknowledge your feelings, soothe yourself to restore your emotional balance, stay connected to yourself and the other person, and set your boundaries.

Here's a great example of everything working together.

This situation happened to Anushka, a graduate student at a major university. She is in a very challenging and rigorous program conducting breast cancer research. Her mentor, a very well-known researcher, confronted her about her commitment to being a scientist because she requested some time off to go see her brother's newborn child. He wrote her a very scathing e-mail questioning her commitment.

Anushka's response to the mentor's e-mail is illuminating.

At first she was anxious and a bit intimidated. But when she took the time to think about what he was saying, instead of reacting impulsively to her anxiety, she centered herself and regained her balance. She didn't give her anxiety privilege! She didn't follow its lead. Here's her written response to him:

> In response to your e-mail, I want to apologize for any misunderstanding. Considering our conversation last week regarding time off, I didn't think you would have a major problem with me taking vacation time to leave a little early on Friday. I would be leaving Friday at 12:30 or 1 p.m., so I would be taking about four hours of vacation time. As for me working over the weekends, I wasn't implying that this time would make up for any vacation time I might take. I was simply notifying you that I have accounted for my experiments and will not be neglecting my work. I don't feel my productivity has ever been a problem in the past. However, if you have concerns over my abilities as a Ph.D. student or a scientist, I would like to discuss this with you in person.
>
> I have to admit that I was hurt by your comments about being a serious and competitive scientist. I feel that I do deliver as a student and a scientist. Working on a weekend is not an unusual event for me and has little to do with whether I take vacation time.
>
> I will be happy to discuss any future days off with you in person as well as notify you of the experiments I have planned around these dates.

Anushka did have a meeting with her mentor and she held on to her center. She didn't let him define her reality, and yet she remained open to his feedback. She left that meeting feeling very good about herself.

Having someone misread us or judge us doesn't have to knock us off balance. We need to always remember that anxiety distorts reality. Our feelings are not an impeccable guide to the truth.

We need to challenge the personal myths that are spawned by emotional dependency. Differences don't need to threaten us or our connection. Embracing and appreciating our differences will ultimately bring us closer together, and not create distance.

So be on the lookout for times when you let other people edit your reality. View these situations as opportunities to hold on to your center. The more you support yourself, the more autonomy you will experience. Conversely, the more you let your emotional dependency influence your behavior, the more you will turn your relationships into emotional prisons.

Learning how to stop taking other people's behavior personally is another step toward holding on to ourselves. Let's discuss this next.

Smart Thing 3
Stop Taking Things Personally

Hopefully it is becoming clear that we achieve emotional sobriety by maintaining our autonomy in relationship to others and circumstances. This does not mean we are cold and calloused or that we avoid people or circumstances. Quite the contrary. We eagerly anticipate interaction with others, because we aren't worried that we will lose ourselves. We have faith in our ability to manage our anxiety or other feelings, whatever they may be. However, as our ability to hold on to our center decreases, we become increasingly more reactive to the input from others. We lose our autonomy. We become guarded and reactive.

As we learned in the last chapter, letting other people edit our reality is one way that emotional dependency manifests itself in our lives. Another way is by taking others' reactions personally. We've all experienced this. A specific look, comment, or action can provide an emotional high or low. We develop a "reflected sense of self" in relationship to others and circumstances. We see the other person's behavior as though it were a mirror reflecting their thoughts or feelings toward us.

This way of interpreting other people's behavior as being "all about us" is a symptom of *emotional fusion*. When we are emotionally dependent, we are driven to seek emotional fusion. To become emotionally sober, we need to work to maintain *emotional differentiation*. This is what I mean when I say we need to stop taking others' reactions personally.

Fusion is very apparent in relationships where one or both partners believe that intimacy is missing unless both partners always feel the same way. The drive for fusion also exists in all types of friendships, though it is more subtle. It's too bad that we seek fusion, because differences in perception and feeling in relationships are normal and healthy, even enriching.

Have you ever enjoyed a dish of tiramisu, that great Italian dessert? It consists of layers of light cake ("ladyfingers"), whipped cream (mascarpone), and cocoa dust, bound together with a touch of espresso. Though each layer is delicious on its own, the delight of this food is the *difference* in the textures and tastes we encounter as we eat them. If we were to mush all the layers of tiramisu into a bowl, we'd get a bland mass of wet dough. But as we encounter the separate layers, we get to enjoy and savor each. At the same time, we take pleasure in the way the flavors and textures work together. This is the joy of that particular dessert. In the same way, there is joy to be found in the differences of individuals in a healthy relationship, whether between friends or lovers. The way the differences are still real and maintained is what makes the whole such a delight.

When we are driven by emotional fusion, we constantly try to mix the flavors together—to fuse everything into one. But seeking emotional fusion rather than connection with differentiation robs us and our relationships of the very things that make them special.

Why do we seek fusion? Because emotional dependency has robbed us of our autonomy and self-esteem; we are dependent on external validation. Our self-esteem is other-validated—it is *based on how other people feel or act toward us*. It's our perceived reputation with others that determines our sense of well-being. Therefore we carefully monitor people for their attitude toward us and for either real or perceived reactions. We tune in to the tone of their voice, their body language, what they say and what they don't say, and how they act or don't act toward us. Our radar is looking for anything and everything that would be either a validation or a threat.

The more differentiated we are, the less reactive we are to other people or circumstances. The more mature we are, the less we take others' reactions personally. The opposite, of course, describes many of us: As our level of differentiation decreases, we become more reactive to other people or circumstances. This means that you can get a rough idea of your level of maturity or differentiation by observing how reactive you are to other people and circumstances. If you find yourself taking things personally all the time, then you are undifferentiated. Do not be alarmed. We are all works in progress. No one among us is perfectly differentiated.

Here's another interesting thing to note: we all have two levels of maturity, a *basic* level of maturity and a *functional* level of maturity. Remember that scale of differentiation of self I discussed earlier? The scale ranged from 0 to 100. Let's say your basic level of maturity or differentiation is 50. If you are under an overwhelming amount of stress, your functional level of maturity may drop to as low as 30 or even 20, and you will be much more reactive to your anxiety and to the behavior of others. You will be taking almost everything personally.

At other times in your life, you may be in the groove, spending a lot of time in the Twelve Step fellowship, or in therapy, or helping others, or being of service in meetings, and your functional level of maturity rises to 70 or even 80. When you are functioning at this level, you will not be nearly as reactive to your feelings or the real or perceived feelings or actions of others.

What's important to remember is that regardless of where our basic level of maturity falls, we can raise our functional level of maturity. We can do this by learning to hold on to ourselves and by developing a solid network of support that includes working with a sponsor on a regular basis, strengthening our relationship with our family, developing friendships in the fellowship, having a home group, working the Steps, working with others (or helping others or being of service in meetings), and possibly working with a therapist, spiritual director, or both. These actions act like a vaccine against the effects of stress and anxiety. The more grounded our recovery, the more resilient we are to the effects of stress.

Let's return to this issue of taking things personally. Here's an example from my personal life. I attended graduate school at the University of California, Davis. It was a unique program. Our training was provided by a graduate group in clinical psychology within the School of Medicine's Department of Psychiatry. Therefore we were allowed to attend seminars for the psychiatric residents. One such seminar was taught by Dr. John Battista. He was a brilliant psychotherapist. In fact, in 1982 he assumed the practice of M. Scott Peck, the author of *The Road Less Traveled*.

I really wanted to learn from Dr. Battista and also impress him. The topic of his seminar was Psychoanalytic Theory. Each student was required to select a paper written by Sigmund Freud and present it for discussion. I chose one that focused on Freud's instinct theory. Freud had always been difficult for me to read and understand, so I spent hours preparing my presentation. I distinctly remember coming to class, thinking, "I am really going to nail this presentation." Not five minutes into it, Dr. Battista interrupted me. It seems I had missed the most important point of the paper. I was humiliated! I took his intervention very personally and felt like I had blown my opportunity to impress him.

When I analyzed my feelings later, I realized that I was only partially upset because I missed the essence of the paper. Yes, that bothered me because I wasn't as smart as I thought I was, but what was even more upsetting was that I imagined that Dr. Battista thought I was stupid. I took his interruption personally.

Later, when I talked to him about what happened, I found out that he didn't think this way at all—it was my projection. (We will talk about how powerful projections are later.) The point I had missed about Freud was in fact very subtle; it was not surprising that I had missed it. Dr. Battista was just doing his job as a teacher and ensuring that we understood what he believed to be most important about this aspect of Freud's ideas.

The interplay of individuality and togetherness is important in every relationship. The balance of these two basic needs becomes skewed, in one direction or the other, when emotional dependency exists. Here's an example of how emotional dependency lends itself to taking things personally in a marriage.

Samantha and Dexter had been married for two years. They were emotionally fused and it was wreaking havoc on their relationship. Dexter could easily tell you what was wrong with his wife, but he wasn't aware of his own emotional fusion. Since the early days of their marriage, he had felt increasingly controlled by Sam and her demands. He loved her very much but was tired of having to constantly reassure her. He responded to her pressure by emotionally distancing himself from her. He would play basketball three nights a week after work. When Sam confronted him about this time away, he told her that he needed exercise. While this was partially true, it wasn't the whole story. He didn't dare tell his wife that he was trying to avoid her endless complaints about how he wasn't meeting her needs. He was tired of hearing what he was doing wrong. He felt trapped, so he withdrew.

The level of stability, cohesiveness, and cooperation in a relationship is strongly affected by the interplay of individuality and togetherness, as we see with Dexter and Sam. Sam took Dexter's avoidance personally, and it made her even more anxious, desiring even greater reassurance. They were caught in a vicious cycle. Sam interpreted Dexter's behavior as unloving and uncaring, and she pressed him for proof that he really cared about her. She interpreted much of Dexter's behavior as "too little" involvement with her, and it automatically triggered actions on her part that were designed to restore a sense of adequate closeness (thus her complaints to Dexter about what he was doing wrong). Dexter interpreted Sam's behavior as "too much" involvement; this triggered actions in him that were designed to restore a sense of adequate separation (his withdrawal and playing basketball). Their emotional dependency made them take each other's behavior personally. Sam felt abandoned by Dexter, and he felt criticized by her.

Even our relationships within AA, NA, or Al-Anon are not immune to these dynamics. For example, Deshan was working with his sponsor, Herb, for about two years. They had a very close relationship. For the past six months, they had spent two hours a week working the Steps. Then Herb got really sick. He was diagnosed with cancer and started a rigorous course of chemotherapy. It was rough going for some time. The chemotherapy was taking its toll: He was fatigued most of the time, had lost a lot of weight and all his hair, and had trouble concentrating and sitting through meetings. Deshan tried to keep in contact with Herb during his chemo, but things weren't the same. Herb didn't have as much energy to give to their relationship. His functioning dropped significantly. Although he knew Herb was sick, Deshan nonetheless felt rejected and abandoned—and then he felt guilty about his feelings because he knew Herb was sick. He reacted to Herb's behavior as though it were a *personal* rejection and abandonment.

Where we focus is where our energy goes. When our energy is focused on how the other person is treating us, or reacting to us, we develop a huge blind spot in our awareness. We are unable to see how we are behaving or acting. We can't see what we are doing that is contributing to the real or perceived problem. When we focus on other people's actions or reactions, it's easy to see how they affect us or what they are doing wrong. But because our focus is on them, our self-awareness becomes dulled and restricted. It's like we are looking at the world through a drinking straw. We don't see our self-centeredness or our distortions. We don't see our egocentricity—that we're acting as if we're the center of the universe. We aren't able to integrate the concept we hear in meetings—"You aren't that important."

So how do we begin to untie the Gordian knot that emotional dependency creates in our life? The guiding principle is to stay connected to the person or situation while simultaneously holding on to yourself. Al-Anon offers great advice in this regard. The Al-Anon newcomer is told, "It's not what they (the alcoholic) are doing to us, it's just what they are doing." What a helpful perspective! We need to realize that we are not the center of the universe. We aren't that important. If you are in a relationship with an alcoholic, you need to realize that they are not drinking because of you! *It's not personal.*

Again from Al-Anon we get another useful perspective: "You didn't cause it (the alcoholism), you can't cure it, and you can't control it." Understanding this concept is relevant not only for the person in a relationship with an alcoholic; it is important for the rest of us too. We need to strive for detachment while simultaneously staying connected. It seems like a paradox, but it's not. We *can* keep our close emotional connection with our partner or friend, without becoming emotionally fused. But there is another consideration that is equally important. Dr. Kempler, a brilliant family therapist and my mentor, stated it this way: "In order to get more personal, you have to stop taking the other person's behavior personally" (1982). Wow, what a profound observation!

We know that intimacy requires really seeing each other. Someone even said that the word *intimacy* breaks down into "in to me you see." But emotional dependency interferes with this process. We react as though everything is about us, rather than understanding and seeing what the person's behavior is saying about them. Let's apply these two useful perspectives to the three examples previously described.

In my personal example, I was so focused on wanting to impress Dr. Battista and dependent on his opinion of me that I left no room for him to be who he was. I completely lost perspective. I didn't even consider that he was in charge of the class and it was his job to ensure that we learned the greatness and limitations of Freud's thoughts. When he interrupted my presentation, I was unable to see that he was doing his job. My emotional dependency prevented me from seeing him.

Sam and Dexter "missed" each other. Sam lacked emotional sobriety, and so she needed constant attention from Dexter. Dexter couldn't see that Sam's pressure on him for constant reassurance was an indication of her emotional dependency. Remember, emotional dependency leads us to falsely conclude that if we are more loved or nurtured, we would be fine. This leads us to expect, and demand, togetherness, because we believe that if someone really loves us, they will meet all our needs. Dr. Virginia Satir (1972), a brilliant family therapist, described it in this way:

One of the truly basic problems is that our society bases the marital relationship almost completely on love and then imposes demands on it that love can never solely fulfill.

If you love me you won't do anything without me.

If you love me you'll do what I say.

If you love me you'll give me what I want.

If you love me you'll know what I want before I ask.

These kinds of practices soon make love into a kind of blackmail, I call the clutch.

Satir's message is incredibly important: More love and attention won't heal our wounds because the wounds weren't caused by a lack of love and attention. They were caused by the emotional atmosphere in our family of origin. They were caused by emotional fusion. When togetherness or individuality is the predominant driving force in a family, then everything that happens in our lives is interpreted along these lines.

Trying to reassure someone who demands reassurance only re-inforces the myth that more closeness is what is needed—as we saw with Sam and Dexter. The opposite is also true. Trying to create more space for someone who demands more independence only re-inforces the myth that more distance is needed. Such solutions don't solve these relationship problems. They only re-create the dynamic that the partners in the relationship grew up with.

If Dexter stopped taking Sam's behavior personally, he would see how her emotional dependence was calling for the increased to-getherness. She was replaying what happened when she was growing up. He would realize that the pressure he was feeling wasn't because of what he was or wasn't doing—it was about Sam and how she learned to deal with her basic need for togetherness. It wasn't that he was failing Sam as a partner. If he could really "get" this at both an intellectual and emotional level, then he could stay connected with Sam and not take what she was saying about him personally.

Sam, on the other hand, never learned how to hold on to herself and meet her own needs. She couldn't see that Dexter was pulling away to avoid losing himself in togetherness. Dexter needed autonomy in the relationship, and the only way he knew how to achieve it was by withdrawing. Yet withdrawal does not help us hold on to ourselves. He withdrew because this is what he learned to do in his family, not because he didn't care for her or that he didn't care enough for her. He felt threatened and needed space, and the only way he could achieve it was by distancing himself emotionally.

If Sam didn't take Dexter's behavior personally, she would have realized that withdrawal is how Dexter learned to deal with his feelings. He, too, was repeating what happened in his family of origin.

What both Sam and Dexter needed to do was to grow up and learn how to stay connected to each other as they searched for a solution. They both needed to increase their level of differentiation.

Deshan took Herb's withdrawal from the sponsor relationship personally. Although he knew that Herb was physically ill, he was unable to see how the illness was taking a toll on Herb psychologically. Herb's cancer brought him face-to-face with his mortality. Herb was pondering his life and what was important to him. He was deep in thought about what he wanted to do with whatever time he had left. If Deshan could have realized this, he could have been emotionally present for Herb. He could have given something back to Herb instead of only taking from him. The only way this would have been possible is if Deshan were to realize that Herb's behavior had nothing to do with him; it was about Herb's own physical, emotional, and spiritual concerns.

The solution to not taking things personally comes from realizing that people don't do things because of who *we* are, but because of who *they* are. When we lose sight of this reality, we only need to check out our perspective. We can ask the person, "I am taking what you said personally. I want to check it out with you. Is this all about me?" While you can use the words that work best for you, the point is to check out your perceptions.

Don't let the fact that we humans are often easily influenced by each other confuse you. It does seem that we do things because of what some other person is doing or not doing. But this is an illusion created by our emotional dependency.

Ultimately we are responsible for how we feel, for our perceptions, and for how we react. As our maturity or differentiation increases, we will experience a greater autonomy in our relationships. We will stay connected to others but not take their behavior personally. We will establish true "I to thou" relationships—relationships based on mutuality.

In such a relationship, *I* relate genuinely to *you*. I stay centered. I remain eye to eye; regardless of what you do, I will maintain a relationship based on mutuality, and there won't be a power differential. The relationship will be horizontal rather than vertical. I will preserve my integrity. I will recognize and respect your individuality and my own individuality. I will join you, but not become fused with you. I will remain autonomous and will usually think before I react.

Growing up and holding on to ourselves is a way of thinking, a perspective, that translates into a way of being that creates our emotional sobriety.

Another important aspect of holding on to ourselves is owning our own projections. This is the focus of the next chapter.

Smart Thing 4

Own Your Projections as an Act of Integrity

Why is it that developing a functional understanding of ourselves is so critical to holding on to ourselves and to emotional sobriety? The reason is that we all have blind spots or holes in our awareness. There are things that are going on within us and around us that we don't see.

As mentioned earlier, Freud observed that, "We are being lived by the forces within us." Yet we are often unaware of the emotional forces operating within us, especially our defense mechanisms. These holes in awareness, these blind spots, prevent us from learning how to respond to our feelings in a more mature and differentiated manner.

Until we become more aware of these emotional forces, they will continue to determine and control our behavior. These emotional forces arise from anxiety or fear, and these emotions impair our judgment. Constrained by anxiety, our perspectives will be limited in their breadth, and therefore we will be misinformed. We won't see the whole picture. In this way, hidden emotional forces prevent us from recovering autonomy and good judgment.

The reality is that we cannot achieve emotional sobriety if we allow hidden emotional forces to control us. Emotional sobriety requires that we be our best self, that we learn to *act* rather than react, that we function from being emotionally centered and informed.

Fritz Perls, M.D., whom I introduced in the introduction, made the following point:

> If we cannot understand ourselves, we can never hope to understand what we are doing, we can never hope to solve our problems, we can never learn to live rewarding lives. However, such understanding of ourselves involves more than the usual intellectual understanding. It requires feeling and sensitivity, too. (1973)

To gain self-understanding, we need to become aware of the psychological mechanisms within us that are usually operating outside of our awareness. One of the most important and common of these mechanisms is *projection.* Our focus here will be on understanding the role of this defense mechanism in our lives: what it does to us, what it does for us, and how it affects our relationship to ourselves and to others. We'll learn about its psychological function and our personal habits of using projection to defend ourselves. We'll also explore what we can do to reverse its effects. This is all necessary information if we are going to take this next step toward our emotional sobriety.

Projection is the act of ascribing to other people the very characteristics in ourselves that we find most unacceptable. Perls defined it this way: "In projection, then, we shift the boundary between ourselves and the rest of the world a little too much in our favor—in a manner that makes it possible to disavow and disown those aspects of our personalities which we find difficult or offensive or unattractive" (1973).

Recall that each of us has an idealized-self—the perfect being we think we need to be in order to be lovable to others. This perfect being has no character "flaws." In order to reduce our anxiety, we have to get rid of the flaws we fear in ourselves, because these flaws make us unlovable. So, we *project* onto other people those attitudes, behaviors, thoughts, and feelings that are unacceptable to our idealized-self. These are things that we would despise ourselves for if we were aware that we behaved in this manner.

Imagine for a moment a gentleman who is living in a house where, unbeknownst to him, all the windows have been replaced with mirrors facing in, toward him. He thinks he is looking out—that he is seeing the world around him as it really is. So, if he is perpetually afraid, he looks out and sees wide eyes and frightened faces. If he is always angry, he sees furrowed brows and frowns. If his face scowls in distrust, he sees suspicion in every window. If he feels greedy and self-absorbed, he looks out and sees selfish and demanding crowds. He is completely convinced that he is seeing the world around him, but he is not. *He is seeing himself.*

So it is for all of us. We see the world as we are, not as it is. This is how projection works, and this is why it is so hard for us to know when we are projecting. Projection is always operating in our lives to one degree or another, which is why it is imperative that we learn about it.

Here's an example of how this mechanism operates in our personalities.

Matt is twenty-eight years old and has been struggling with opioid dependence for over eight years. He has never been married and lives with his seventy-five-year-old grandmother. Matt doesn't trust anyone. He thinks everyone is out to get him or take advantage of him. He is highly suspicious of other people's motives. He believes everyone has malicious and selfish intentions. The world according to

Matt is a dangerous place, filled with con artists who are constantly trying to take advantage of him or suck him dry or rip him off.

If you were a fly on the wall and observed Matt over the past sixteen years, this would be an accurate description of how Matt functions. As a kid, he often stole things from friends—money, toys, baseball cards, clothes—just about anything was fair game if he wanted it. He took advantage of relationships and friendships. He was angry because he felt that life had dealt him a bad hand, and therefore it was each man for himself. Matt's father had abandoned him and his mother at Matt's birth. As a result, Matt felt entitled to more than he got from life, and he exploited this position with a vengeance. He was a taker and rarely gave anything in return. As a high school student, he cheated to pass classes. He took advantage of the kindness and generosity of fellow students and faculty.

As a young adult, he surreptitiously gained access to his grandmother's bank accounts and credit cards. Over the past eight years he had stolen more than $100,000 from her to buy OxyContin and heroin.

Matt didn't take responsibility for any of his rotten behavior. He minimized his transgressions. He felt justified taking things from others; he glorified himself as a kind of Robin Hood. When confronted about the indecency of stealing money from his grandmother, he said, "It's a part of my inheritance—so it really doesn't matter. I'm just spending my inheritance a little sooner. She won't miss it or need it. She has plenty of money." Matt persistently rationalized his behavior and projected the exact nature of his wrongs onto the world. What he didn't realize was that he believed everyone functioned like him. He could not see that he was projecting his attitude onto the world and everyone in it. In the house that Matt had built, all the mirrored windows revealed exploitive people.

Projection is not always as dramatic as Matt's example of para-
noia suggests. It operates in subtle ways too. Take Heather, for example. Heather didn't think that her boyfriend, Jian, was interested
in the problem she was having with her mother or with what she was
going through. She complained about this often to Jian, and they
would get into heated arguments about it. Jian insisted that he did
care and was perplexed and baffled at Heather's complaints. He kept
asking her to give him examples. She couldn't, but said, "It is just a
feeling I get when I talk to you."

As we explored Heather's perceptions in therapy, we discovered
that Heather had not shown any interest in how her behavior and
her problems with her mother were affecting Jian and their relationship. She wasn't interested in Jian or his feelings at this moment.
What she wanted was for Jian to be interested in her.

Jian actually did care about Heather's problem and could provide many specific examples where he had demonstrated his concern.
What was happening between Heather and Jian was that Heather
was projecting onto Jian how she was treating him. Heather's ideal
self was a person who was very caring and giving. But during this
time of difficulty with her mother, she really did need lots of care
and concern from Jian—she needed to be totally "selfish." She did
not have mental energy to care about him. Yet this selfishness was
unacceptable to Heather, regardless of the circumstances. Although
Heather didn't want to give anything to Jian, she didn't dare admit
this. Therefore Jian became the depository for the part of her that
she couldn't accept about herself. It would have been unthinkable
for Heather to tell Jian, "Right now I am not interested in you and
how this is affecting you. I want to focus of all of my attention on
this situation with my mother and I want you to do the same." In
the house that Heather had built, the windows, temporarily, showed

a Jian who was demanding and self-absorbed. This was exactly how Heather felt about herself and was what she wanted. It just didn't fit with her ideal self.

I hope it is becoming clear that often what we believe to be unacceptable may actually be perfectly acceptable. Heather wanted to have Jian's attention, without having to be concerned about him in return. This happens at times in *every* relationship. It's not a problem for limited periods of time—it is actually a benefit of a close relationship. It only becomes a problem if we become stuck in that position. But this wasn't okay for Heather. It is not who she thought she *should* be. So she disowned that part of her and projected it onto Jian.

Here are some other ways we may project our feelings onto others:

- If you think everyone is a liar, it probably means that you aren't owning how you lie.
- If you think life is unfair, it likely means that you aren't fair, but you aren't taking responsibility for being unfair.
- If you see everyone as angry, it probably means that you are projecting your own anger onto the world.
- If you see everyone as being seductive, then it may mean that you are disowning your sexual desires.
- If you see everyone as stubborn, it is likely that you are stubborn and you don't want to face it.
- If you don't like how arrogant someone is, it is likely that you are disowning your own arrogance.
- If you see someone as demanding and insensitive of other people's feelings, then you are likely disowning your own insensitivity and demandingness.
- If you think most people are self-centered or narcissistic,

then it is likely that you are projecting your self-centeredness and narcissism onto others.

- If you see people as judgmental, then it is likely that you are judgmental and not taking responsibility for it.

The list can go on and on and on.

Hugh Prather, in a thoughtfully written book called *Notes to Myself* (1970), commented,

> If I feel aversion toward someone, if I find myself ignoring or turning away from someone in a group, I am probably avoiding within myself what this person represents that is true about me. If something that you do rankles me, I can know that your fault is my fault too. The criticism that hurts the most is the one that echoes my own self-condemnation.

Hugh's insight provides us with one way to start reclaiming those things we are projecting.

So here's the exercise I'd like you to try. Take out a piece of paper and make three columns on it. In the first column, list the top five people you can't stand, people that you really don't like. In the next column, take a rigorous inventory of their character defects. Leave no stone unturned! Write down all their despicable traits. In the third column, ask yourself, "Is this the way I behave? Is this my feeling?" Write down your response. Then try it on for size.

Here's an example. Let's say in the first column you mentioned a person you work with, and you noted that one of the things that you can't stand about her is that she is two-faced, that she is a phony. Ask yourself if you behave this way too. If you aren't certain, then try it on for size. Say, "I am a phony" or "I am two-faced." My experience has been that if there is some truth to the statement, you will feel it in your gut. You will recognize that a part of you behaves this way too.

Your work in the third column is how you will begin to recognize that the windows in your house are really mirrors. The process of coming to grips with the list in the third column is the process of opening the windows so you can see the world as it is.

Remember, we don't change by trying to be something we are not; we change when we become who we are. This paradox is at the core of personal transformation.

- When we admit to lying, we take the first step toward honesty.
- When we admit that we want to win all the time, we take the first step toward cooperation.
- When we admit our unreasonableness, we take the first step toward becoming reasonable.
- When we admit our arrogance, we take the first step toward humility.
- When we own how judgmental we are, we become less judgmental and more tolerant.
- When we admit our emotional dependency, we take the first step toward emotional sobriety—toward growing up.

In the very same way, owning our projections is critical to emotional sobriety: We have to admit to projecting before we can take the first step toward ceasing projection. This step helps us stay emotionally centered and reduces our blind spots. If we can own our projections, then we can truly admit when we are wrong. We can stop blaming others for what we are doing.

Owning our projections helps us hold on to our individuality and autonomy because it reduces our reactivity. When we own something we are projecting, then we can act on the situation rather than react to it. We throw open the mirrored windows of our self-made houses and discover that the scowls of fear or anger or suspicions or selfishness or judgment we'd seen were actually the expressions on our own faces. We begin to see who we are, and simultaneously we see other people as they really are—which is one of the great gifts of emotional sobriety.

Let us now turn to the next thing you can do to hold on to yourself. In the next chapter we will explore the importance of confronting yourself for the sake of your integrity.

Smart Thing 5
Confront Yourself for the Sake of Your Integrity

Let's take a moment to recap what we have discussed so far.

Emotional sobriety is about growing up and learning to stand on our own two feet. To achieve emotional sobriety, we have to un-hook our emotional dependency and learn how to maintain our autonomy in relations with other people or circumstances. The first step toward this goal is to identify our emotional dependency and its consequent demands. We learned techniques to stop letting other people edit our own reality and ways to stop taking things so personally. We also looked at how the defense mechanism of projection interferes with our emotional sobriety, and how to reclaim and own what we have been projecting. Now we are ready to take the next step in unraveling the emotional dependency in our lives.

Recovery requires rigorous honesty. In order to be honest with ourselves, we need to quit running from the truth. We need to stop avoiding our pain, our fears, or our anxiety. It is hard to admit that our lives are full of mistakes and self-deception. But they are, and once we accept this painful truth, our thinking shifts dramatically.

We first began to unveil our self-deception in the beginning of our recovery when we admitted that "Our problems are of our own making." By confronting ourselves with this reality, we came face-to-face with the fatal nature of our condition. This very admission, though painful and disquieting, made recovery possible. We went from blaming people, places, and things for our troubles to accepting total responsibility for the mess in our lives. We started looking at life through a new pair of glasses instead of a drinking straw.

In order to achieve real peace of mind and emotional sobriety, we need to continue to confront ourselves. Many people say that recovery is like peeling back the layers of an onion. One layer after another comes off, but only if we continue to confront ourselves. If we want emotional sobriety, self-confrontation needs to be ongoing, not intermittent.

Therefore we need to construct a *personal crucible* of self-confrontation. In this crucible, we stop avoiding ourselves and stop focusing on the faults of others. We confront our own personal issues and identify the ways we are contributing to our own unhappiness. When we do this, we begin to grow up and self-differentiate.

What are the things we need to confront ourselves about? Well, the usual suspects are our character defects, our shortcomings, and those we have hurt. These are important issues to face, there's no doubt about it, but we also need to confront ourselves in one other area. We need to be able to see and identify our behavioral patterns and their emotional themes. This is revealed most clearly when we examine the conflicts or struggles we have with others.

This is a tall order, and many ask, "Why do we have to go to such trouble? Isn't there an easier way to achieve emotional sobriety?"

No, there isn't. We go through these troubles because they ensure that we establish and maintain a sense of humility, a prerequisite for recovery. We cannot achieve humility without authenticity, without facing who we really are. And the way we find out who we are is by confronting ourselves.

Yet the end goal of self-confrontation is about more than seeing ourselves as we really are. It's about figuring out how our behaviors differ from what we know to be right, and then changing our behaviors so they harmonize with our best self. When we see ourselves as we really are, we can begin to align our behaviors with our recovery, our values, our principles, our deepest desires, and our basic needs like self-actualization.

This is the very definition of integrity. Integrity is wholeness. It is the result of living an authentic life, of "true speaking." *Integrity, wholeness, authenticity, true speaking*—these are all words we have to describe a person whose actions, values, beliefs, and innermost "best self" work in complete harmony.

When we develop this new, authentic relationship with ourselves, we will be open to learning as much as we can from our experiences. We will then be able to extract the unresolved personal issues embedded in our emotional reactions and in our conflict with others. Here's a case in point.

Elliot had been sober for almost ten years. He was now thirty-eight years old and had been married for five years. His wife wanted a child. He loved his wife very much, but he wasn't sure that he wanted to be a father. Initially he refused to talk with her about the issue, but it was too important for her to let it go. She approached him in a very loving and yet firm way. "Honey, I know you love me and that our relationship is important to you. At least I hope it is. I have told you how important it is for me to have a child with you, but it's even more important to me that we can discuss this issue together, openly and honestly. I imagine I may feel threatened by some of your feelings, but I will deal with these feelings. I'd like you to come and see a therapist with me so that we can get some help in working through this impasse."

Elliot's recovery was solid. Deep down he didn't like how he was avoiding the issue of parenthood. He knew he needed to confront this issue sooner or later. He chose to do it sooner. He told his wife he would go to therapy.

His willingness was evident in our first session. Elliot owned that he had been avoiding his wife because he had been avoiding himself. He suspected that there were a bunch of unresolved issues that he would have to finally face if he opened up Pandora's box. He was right. There were.

I always respect a person's resistance, so I asked Elliot to explore these feelings further before we addressed anything else. This proved to be very productive. Elliot said he was afraid he would lose his wife if he didn't agree to give her a child. He said that he pressured himself to please her regardless of his feelings. So he *moved toward* her. (Recall that "moving toward" was one of the ways we have of continuing our emotional dependence and avoiding self-differentiation, which blocks emotional sobriety.)

But Elliot was also afraid of what he might learn about himself if he honestly explored his feelings. He knew he had many unresolved feelings toward his father. As we discussed these feelings, he realized that he had been avoiding these issues with his father for his entire adult life. He suspected that this is what caused him problems with his male boss and with several teachers he had in college. He concluded that he was selling himself and his wife short by continuing to avoid these issues. He decided to finally confront himself and deal with whatever was uncovered or discovered. He created his crucible of self-confrontation—a brave act indeed.

Elliot explored many issues over the next several months. First he looked at his selfishness and then his concern that he wouldn't be a very good father. He liked doing whatever he wanted to do, whenever he wanted to do it. His wife was really supportive of his recovery and his fellowship, so he had a lot of freedom in their relationship. He was afraid this would change if they had a child. But he was also concerned that he didn't have a good role model to be a father.

His relationship with his father had always been strained and marked by distance and pain. He always felt that he was a disappointment to his father—a feeling that was based partially on reality and was partially imagined. As he talked about these feelings, he sobbed. He had never cried about this relationship, though he had felt much sadness and grief. His wife was visibly moved by his vulnerability and honesty. By confronting himself, Elliot became aware of many unresolved issues that needed to be addressed before he could consider embracing the idea of having a child.

Elliot eventually invited his father into a therapy session. It was an incredibly powerful experience. When Elliot talked about his dilemma, his father opened up too. They had a very important personal conversation that was long overdue. Elliot's father revealed that he also felt unprepared and inadequate when he became a father. He cried about not being closer to Elliot and expressed regret about treating Elliot in the same critical way that his own father treated him. Without any prompting, he turned to Elliot and, with tears in his eyes, asked him for forgiveness. Elliot reached out and hugged his father, holding him like he had never done before. This created a welcomed closeness that they never dreamed possible.

Elliot turned out to be a great dad. He now has three wonderful children whom he genuinely enjoys. Elliot confronted himself *for the sake of his own integrity.* He wanted to be the best person he could possibly be. And as a result of his self-confrontation, he was able to wholeheartedly embrace parenthood. He also became much closer to his own father, a completely unexpected benefit. This often happens; confronting ourselves for the right reason creates an atmosphere that encourages those close to us to respond in kind. This outcome occurs because we are not pushing an agenda on anybody other than ourselves. It's attraction rather than promotion.

Most of us have set up elaborate defenses against seeing our true selves. To confront ourselves honestly, then, we need to surrender our favorite ways of avoiding ourselves. We need to quit enabling ourselves and deceiving ourselves into thinking we are all right.

It's not easy to surrender our defenses, and to do so puts us at risk. We instinctively know that as we begin to confront ourselves, we will see unpleasant truths and, worse, will have to change! In fact, that's why we avoid self-confrontation.

Therefore, we need to set up some *positive conditions* to ensure that we will not abandon ourselves during this process. We need to learn (1) how to support ourselves, (2) how to soothe ourselves, and (3) how to have compassion for ourselves and what we see when we stop our self-deception. Let's explore each of these conditions.

Self-Support

What is self-support? How do I learn to support myself in a healthy way? How do I support myself when I don't like what I have done? How do I support myself when I don't feel worthy? These are a few of the questions we ask ourselves.

In order to be self-supportive, we need to give up our ideas about who we should be. Remember, our idealized-self demanded that we act a certain way. The idealized-self is based on absolutes. There are no gray areas. We either are okay or we are not. There is nothing in between. Pride and self-hatred ensure that we live according to the dictates of this tyrant. If we behave like we should, we reward ourselves with pride. If we do not live up to its perfectionistic specifications, we punish ourselves with self-deprecation and self-hate. We despise ourselves for being other than who we think we should be.

Self-support is the ability to encourage ourselves to face ourselves as we *are,* without condemnation. Self-support is based on self-acceptance. When we accept ourselves as we are, in this moment, it means that we embrace ourselves without judgment. Self-acceptance leads to growth and self-esteem.

Let's say that I am unhappy with how I just dealt with a situation at work. My boss crossed a boundary with me, and I didn't stand up for myself because I was afraid of not being liked and losing my job. Here's what my self-talk would sound like if I was "shoulding" on myself.

> What a wimp I am. I am such a coward. I should be more assertive. When am I going to stand up for myself? I am sick and tired of being weak and pathetic!

I would read myself the riot act. Most of us respond to a personal shortcoming or failure in a ruthless and vicious manner similar to this.

Yet the idea that it will help me become a better person if I attack and beat myself up is ridiculous, isn't it? The concept that if we spare the rod we spoil the child is nonsense. It doesn't work. *No one learns under these conditions.* Self-scolding does nothing to unpack the lessons from our experience. In fact, more often than not, we're so busy telling ourselves how bad we are that we miss the lesson.

There is another reason why we are so ruthless with ourselves. This kind of self-deprecating response fools us into thinking that we are doing something about the problem. All we are doing is deceiving ourselves. We are not critically or objectively examining our experience.

To avoid losing the lesson of our experience, we need to support ourselves when we confront a personal failure or face a shortcoming. If I was supportive of myself, I would say something more like this:

> It is good that I am unhappy about what just happened with my boss. This is not who I want to be. I see clearly now how much difficulty I have asserting myself. I need to stop running away from this shortcoming and face it. I know I am afraid of being disliked, so I swallow my feelings. I can see that I do this a lot in all my relationships. It is good that I am unhappy with this part of myself. I am tired of living like this. It's time to get some help. I'll start by giving my sponsor a call and talking to him about it.

As this example illustrates, one key factor in supporting ourselves is to stop beating ourselves up. Instead, we can discover the lesson inherent in our difficulty and create a condition that is likely to result in change.

Self-Soothing

Self-soothing consists of comforting ourselves when we are unhappy with what we are seeing about ourselves. But how can we be all right with ourselves in such a situation? How can we comfort ourselves? The answer lies in maintaining perspective. For example, it is knowing that even though I have made a mistake, I am not myself a mistake. It means surrendering the idealized-self that wants to be perfect. It means accepting that "no one among us has been able to maintain anything like perfect adherence to these principles." And that we are "willing to grow along spiritual lines" (AA 2001, 60).

I remember working with a young man, Mohammed, who was in the early stages of his recovery. He was struggling with a dream he had that he called a nightmare. He dreamt that he was at the beach surfing with his girlfriend. He caught a wave slightly ahead of her. When he glanced back to see how she was doing, he thought he saw her gesturing to someone on the beach. He turned to look at the beach and saw his girlfriend's ex-boyfriend gesturing to her. He became incredibly uncomfortable and angry and then woke up.

Dreams are a combination of experiences we have in our daily life along with the struggles we are having integrating various parts of our personalities or experiences. Mohammed was having trouble accepting the jealousy he was experiencing. For him, jealousy meant that you were weak and somehow inadequate. He couldn't accept what he was feeling so instead he blamed his girlfriend. Thus, in the dream, he made her wrong and became angry and judgmental. "How dare you act that way. You are really messed up. You are playing games with me." He *had* to make her wrong because that made it okay for him to be angry and upset, and for him to continue to avoid owning his jealousy and projections.

As he discussed what happened in the dream, he never once mentioned the word *jealousy*. This revealed how deeply committed he was to avoiding this feeling. When I pointed out that he avoided labeling his feeling as jealousy, he stopped and said that he didn't want to feel jealous—that being jealous was wrong. I responded incredulously. I told him that I always thought that feeling jealous indicated that the other person was important to you. That being jealous wasn't wrong, in itself; it was a matter of how you coped with the feeling. Mohammed had an epiphany. He realized that the feeling was okay; it only became a problem when he denied it and tried to control his partner's behavior to ensure he would never have to feel jealous.

This shift in perspective allowed Mohammed to soothe himself and accept feeling jealous instead of avoiding it. Self-soothing can take the form of self-talk that accepts and encourages, such as

"Feeling jealous is only human. I can forgive myself and learn from this experience." Sometimes a small change in our perspective can make a huge difference.

Self-Compassion

Self-compassion is the result of accepting that we are imperfect—that while we may strive for perfection, we will never reach it. It's based on the realization that we come to our self-destructive behavior legitimately. We did the best we could at the time, but our problematic behavior was based on limited information and so was itself limited.

This perspective becomes the foundation for self-compassion. We know that we are generally doing the best we can. There is no exception to this fact. Therefore, if we didn't handle a situation as well as we'd like to, it's because we didn't know how. It's because something is missing in our life experience. We are either ignorant and need better information, or we are sabotaging who we want to be with some old ideas—ideas we have swallowed whole without any critical examination. Whatever the case, we need to stop berating ourselves for our problems and get on with unpacking their lessons.

When we support ourselves, soothe ourselves, and have compassion for ourselves, our ability to be honest with ourselves deepens. People on this journey often say that the better they feel about themselves, the more they can see the worst in themselves. Though it may sound ironic, the person who said, "The better I feel about myself, the worse I get," was revealing a deep truth: It is safer to admit and correct our shortcomings when we have a core faith in our goodness.

Emotional dependency activates many different kinds of defense mechanisms, many methods to keep us from facing the truth about ourselves. We project what we are doing, we rationalize it, we intellectualize it, we try to undo it, or we pretend it didn't happen. We have dozens of magic tricks up our sleeves, but we need to stop using them if we are going to grow up emotionally.

Ulterior Motives

There is one other area I want to explore before leaving this subject. It's how emotional dependency can negatively influence our motive for confronting ourselves. It's almost like we regress into an "I will show you mine if you show me yours" mentality. We end up confronting ourselves because we want to have some kind of effect on our partner or on our reputations rather than confronting ourselves because it is intrinsically rewarding.

Here's an example of how this manifests itself in our relationships. Sergio has been sober for eight years. He is engaged to Maria, who has also been clean and sober for six years. They have been dating for two years and recently decided to get married. They both wanted premarital counseling, which is why they contacted me for an appointment.

In our first session, I asked each of them to discuss what they were most concerned about, what has given them the most trouble in their relationship. They both identified the same area, related to how the Tenth Step is worked in their relationship. The Tenth Step reads, "Continued to take personal inventory and when we were wrong promptly admitted it."

Maria is very conscientious about "promptly admitting" when she is wrong in her interactions with Sergio. She tends to be highly reactive to her anxiety and at times will attack Sergio instead of telling him about how anxious she is feeling. For instance, about two weeks before the appointment, they attended a concert at a large sports arena. As they were approaching their car afterward, several young men passed by. They were loud and obnoxious, and it seemed like they were drunk or high. Maria got scared and quickly opened the door and got in the car. As soon as Sergio sat down, she barked at him to lock the doors and then started to criticize him for being insensitive to her feelings. He didn't like how she was talking to him and he told her to shut up.

In about ten minutes, she regained her composure and realized that she was wrong when she attacked him. So she told him that she was sorry for how she had treated him. And then she waited for Sergio to apologize as well. But he didn't, and this really bothered her. She confronted him about it when they got home and told him that he wasn't "working a very good program."

This is that "I will show you mine if you show me yours" mentality that is spawned by our emotional dependency. Maria expected Sergio to work the Tenth Step the way she did, by "promptly" making amends for his behavior. What she didn't say to him was that she wanted him to do it her way, according to her time schedule. Sergio realized he was wrong for telling Maria to shut up, but he wasn't ready to make amends just yet. He needed some time to get perspective. He said, "If I did it because she wanted me to, it wouldn't have been sincere." I found that a thoughtful remark. He was trying to hold on to his integrity, but Maria didn't see this dimension of Sergio's behavior, and he failed to communicate his need to Maria. Instead, Sergio reacted by withdrawing and resenting her pressure. This was not the first time this happened but was, unfortunately, a well-established pattern in their relationship.

What Maria lost sight of was her need to work the Steps for the sake of her own recovery. If Sergio works the Steps in the same way, that is fine, but it can't be a requirement. Maria needs to make amends to keep her integrity, to work her program, to keep her side of the street clean. When she places the expectation on Sergio that he should respond in kind, she is demanding that he do things according to her vision. She is also reliving what happened in her family of origin. This is exactly what her mother and father expected of her.

This is what Bill Wilson admitted to in his letter reprinted in the introduction. He realized that when people or circumstances didn't comply with his demands, he got angry and tried to manipulate the situation or person to adhere to his rules. This isn't healthy, no matter what kind of trick we use to make our demands seem reasonable. A wolf dressed up in sheep's clothing is still a wolf. Whether Maria accuses Sergio of not working the program, or of not being considerate, or of being selfish, or of not really loving her, it's all in the service of pressuring Sergio to do things according to her specifications.

Consciously, Maria was trying to be closer to Sergio. This is what she learned in her family about togetherness. But we do not get closer by demanding that our partner (or anyone else, for that matter) follow our set of rules. For a relationship to work, we need to discard these "hobbling demands," these unreasonable expectations. There has to be room enough for two in a relationship, and that means the rules must go.

Now I am not saying that Maria can't have a personal set of rules that guide *her* behavior. In fact, this is the kind of rule that *does* work in relationships. We can have any rule or principle that we think is helpful or useful, but only if this rule applies exclusively to our behavior. We don't have the right to expect others to live by our standards. If they do wish to cooperate with us because they want to, that's fine. But it can't be expected.

If Maria had confronted herself and made amends for the right reason, the entire relationship dynamic would change. Then she would have been focused on her own recovery, her own Tenth Step, and her own emotional sobriety. She would have confronted herself and made appropriate changes *for the sake of her own integrity*, not to "earn" some sort of quid pro quo amends from Sergio.

When we take total responsibility for our recovery, we confront ourselves for the sake of our integrity. We don't depend on the outcome for our reward. Our reward comes from taking the right action. This is the best and most stable motivation for our recovery. This kind of motivation makes it possible for us to stay the course regardless of the circumstances in our lives, whether we are successful or have experienced a failure, through health or sickness, through pain or joy, through hardships or times of plenty. When we are committed to recovery, we will continue traveling the road to recovery no matter what.

Remember, we need to do what we are doing for *ourselves*, not to get into one's favor or get a slap on the back. This is one of the lessons we learned if we worked Step Nine and made amends to the people we hurt. We made amends to come to peace with ourselves. If the person we wronged accepted our apology and our offer to right the wrong, and then forgave us, then what a wonderful bonus. But we didn't make amends to get their forgiveness; we made amends to clean up our side of the street.

Another practice that helps us hold on to ourselves is to develop a healthy perspective about ourselves and about life. This is what we will explore next.

Smart Thing 6
Stop Pressuring Others to Change, and Instead Pressure Yourself to Change

As we build a set of principles that will help us grow up emotionally and differentiate ourselves from others, there is nothing more important than the principle discussed in the last chapter and the principle we are going to discuss now. Emotional sobriety is about learning how to keep our emotional balance regardless of what is going on around us. As you have seen, one way we facilitate the development of this ability is through self-confrontation. Self-confrontation helps us identify our personal issues, our shortcomings, our stuck points, and our working points. When we confront ourselves for the sake of our own integrity, we stop avoiding our personal issues. In essence, we stop dodging ourselves and instead focus on identifying the patterns and themes in our lives, extracting from them our unresolved personal issues so we can focus our efforts on growing up.

One way we have avoided looking at ourselves is by externalizing the responsibility for our unhappiness, for our failures, and even for our addiction. We blame others for our troubles, for our low self-esteem, for our frustrations, for how we feel or don't feel, or for how we react. This mentality led us to believe that if conditions were different, *we* would be different. We become obsessed with "If only . . ."

- If only my parents would have been more loving or less abusive, I would have a better life today.
- If only my father or mother weren't an alcoholic, I wouldn't be an addict today.
- If only my boss recognized my talents and efforts, I would have a better job and make more money.
- If only I were taller and more attractive, I would have more self-esteem.
- If only I had more opportunities, I would be more successful.
- If only I had a better body, I would be more attractive and happier.
- If only I had more money, I would be happier.
- If only my partner were more sensitive or expressed his or her feelings better, we would have a better relationship.
- If only my sponsor had more time, I would be able to work the Steps faster.
- If only men weren't such jerks, I would have a better relationship with them.
- If only women were more logical, I could deal with our conflicts much better.
- If only I had more time, then I could do what I really want.
- If only _____ (you fill in the blank), I would be _____.

The list can go on and on ad nauseam. We can get caught up in the futile blame game for the rest of our lives.

Lest I be misunderstood, I want to clarify a couple of things.

First of all, *there is some truth* to the "if things were different" hypothesis. It's true that if certain experiences in our lives were different, we would be different. But while this is true, it is also eventually irrelevant. We experienced what we experienced for whatever reasons. This is our life, our cross to bear, so to speak. Some say this is our karma. It really doesn't matter what explanation we have for why these things happened; the reality is that they happened. We came to our suffering legitimately. The most relevant question we have to ask ourselves is what are we willing to do about it.

Second, I don't mean to ridicule or minimize anyone's suffering or pain. Life is difficult and anything but smooth and easy. Many of us have been traumatized and hurt along the way. Recognizing our pain and traumas, and dealing with these feelings or experiences, is extremely important in recovery. But that's not the issue I am addressing here. What I am objecting to is using these things to justify why we continue to be unhappy or don't feel better about ourselves or why we relapse. This type of thinking is self-destructive and is a real dirty trick that we are playing on ourselves. Regardless of what has happened in our lives, we can become clean and sober; we can become the person we want to be.

Dr. Viktor Frankl, in his important book *Man's Search for Meaning*, said it this way: "The way in which man accepts his fate and all the suffering it entails, the way he takes up his cross, gives him ample opportunity—even under the most difficult circumstances—to add deeper meaning to his life" (1959, 76).

Please don't misinterpret any of what I am saying to mean that we can completely become our idealized-self, because we can never pull off that feat. What we can do is move toward becoming more of who we really are and less of who we imagine we should be. We know from more than one hundred years of therapy and from more than seventy-five years of Alcoholics Anonymous that this outcome is within reach. There is hope and help, as long as we have the capacity to be honest with ourselves.

Honesty is the foundation for self-confrontation. But the truth will only set us free if we have the courage to act on it. We must realize that the "if only" formula is part of the problem, not the solution. We will never develop emotional sobriety if it is dependent on people or circumstances—especially people and circumstances from our past. If our emotional sobriety requires anything other than our efforts right here and right now, we will never grow up. This explains why we need to shift our focus. Remember, where we focus is where our energy goes. If we are focused on the "if onlys" in our lives, our life energy will follow and, then, won't be available for more constructive efforts.

Hopefully you are asking yourself something like, "Okay, Doc, I am convinced that I need to focus my attention on myself, but where do I start?" This is a great question. In the previous chapter, I suggested that you construct your own personal crucible. If you were fearless and thorough in your self-confrontation, you were able to extract and identify your unresolved personal issues, the ones embedded in your conflicts or in your emotional dependency. These are the issues you need to focus on in your recovery. Here are some general guidelines for this work:

- If you are in a partnership, stop working on your relationship and instead focus on yourself. Stop trying to make your partner listen to you, or validate you, or accept you. Instead, start listening to yourself. Focus on learning how to validate yourself and accept yourself. Focus on learning to be self-supportive.

- If you are dissatisfied in your job, stop focusing on what is wrong with it or your fellow employees and instead focus on yourself. Stop hoping that they will function better, and instead focus on how you can start functioning better. Focus on being your best self regardless of what is happening at work.

- If you are attending a Twelve Step meeting that isn't living up to your expectations, stop focusing on what is wrong with the meeting. Instead, shift your focus to what you can do to sweeten the pot. Focus on bringing to the meeting what is missing.
- If you are working with a Twelve Step newcomer and they aren't working the program according to your wishes, stop focusing on what they are doing and instead focus on doing something different with them.

I am suggesting that you let the best of yourself run the show. Then, every time that you fall short, you pull yourself up. Don't wait for someone else to put pressure on you; confront yourself. Take yourself to task, not punitively, but compassionately and firmly. It's time to stop letting your "King Baby" run the show.

"Putting pressure on yourself" sounds good, but how do we do that? The answers surround us. There are at least one hundred times as many ways to pressure ourselves as there are people in the world. Extract from your experiences the next development task for your growth. Can you do this alone, without help? Perhaps not, but you need to define the work by yourself. For example, I still remain in contact with my sponsor and turn to him for help whenever I hit a stuck point in recovery. I have turned outside the program for help with my unresolved issues too. I have spent many hours in therapy with different therapists at various times in my recovery. I have also attended personal growth workshops and retreats, and I have consumed hundreds of self-help books. It has all been useful, even if it has only helped clarify what kind of help I didn't need.

I encourage you to be open and willing to experiment. Try on different therapies or different therapists. Go to a couple of different retreats. Work the Steps if you haven't, or start working them again if you've stopped. Work with a new sponsor if you're in a rut with your current one. Seek out spiritual direction. Be open to new experiences. For answers to unresolved issues, look in different directions than you have in the past. It's even a good idea to reconsider ideas you have rejected in the past. The point is to keep your options open.

Dr. Nathaniel Branden, author of *The Six Pillars of Self-Esteem*, has a sign over the door in his office that says, "NO ONE IS COMING" (2010). The message he is urging his patients to understand is that the quality of their life is dependent upon what they do or don't do. No one is coming to rescue them from their fate. It's up to them.

Like Branden, I am offering suggestions to help us get a more accurate picture of ourselves and help us build up the courage and motivation to change the things we can.

No one among us is perfect. We are all works in progress. Here is a summary of some ways to put what I've been talking about into practice:

- Stop avoiding yourself.
- Listen to yourself rather than demand that other people listen to you.
- Validate yourself instead of manipulating other people to validate you.
- Support yourself instead of expecting other people to support you.
- Accept yourself instead of demanding that other people accept you the way you are.
- Extract from your emotional reactions the unresolved issues in your life and get to work on resolving them.

- Remind yourself that you are doing these things for the sake of your integrity. Your improved self-esteem is your reward.
- Strive to be the best of you and let the best of you run the show.

These ideas are simple, and success with one inevitably leads to the next. Yet, though simple, these ideas are not easy to integrate into our lives. For most of our lives we have been developing bad emotional and mental habits—especially the "if only" habit. It will take time and practice to unlearn them and replace them with more useful and fruitful options.

Do not get discouraged. No one changes all of these things overnight. The point is to be willing and open to a new way of being.

We now turn our attention to developing a healthier attitude toward ourselves.

Smart Thing 7
Develop a Healthy Perspective Toward Yourself, Your Feelings, and Your Emotional Themes

Our quest for emotional sobriety returns us again and again to the same goal: finding ways to hold on to ourselves. This chapter focuses on the *relationship* we have with ourselves. The right type of relationship with ourselves can provide the foundation for holding on to ourselves.

Now it may seem odd to think about having a relationship with ourselves, but we do. We are either supportive of ourselves or critical of ourselves. We sometimes like ourselves and at other times hate ourselves. There are times when we are proud of ourselves and other times when we are ashamed of ourselves.

I noted in the introduction that self-esteem expert Dr. Nathaniel Branden says that our self-esteem is based on the kind of reputation we have with ourselves. For most of us, that reputation is not conducive to holding on to ourselves. But it can be if we develop a healthier perspective on ourselves, our feelings, and our emotional themes.

Our false-self is based on a set of absolute standards. These manifest themselves as dictates. They tell us what we should do, how we ought to behave, and what we are supposed to feel. These rules govern our behavior, our experience with ourselves, and our interaction with others. If we behave the way we think we should, we reward ourselves by feeling pride. If we don't behave as we "should," we punish ourselves by feeling shame or self-hate.

The false-self is a tyrant. Father Richard Rohr, a noted speaker and author on spirituality and well-being, called it the "Imperial Self" (1992, 198). It controls our actions and demands perfect adherence to its rules. We must *surrender* to shatter our reliance on our false-self and "deconstruct" this "Imperial Self." This process has been referred to by Bill Wilson as "deflation at depth" (Kurtz 1979, 21). This psychological shift is quite remarkable. Here are some of the major personal transformations of recovery that begin with this shift.

- The false-self is focused on *having*; recovery is concerned with *being*.
- The false-self wants *control*; recovery is about *letting go* of control and *trusting* the process.
- The false-self wants *perfection*; recovery is about *progress.*
- The false-self *rejects* our true-self and *alienates* us from it; recovery is focused on *renewing our relationship* with our lost true-self.

What is normal and okay for the false-self is not really normal and okay. We've just fooled ourselves into believing its myths. The hidden truth is that the false-self is unreasonable, ruthless, and relentless in its pursuit of perfection. When we buy into the idea that we should be perfect, we hold ourselves to an impossible standard.

Think of it this way: Perfectionism created the wires we used to bonsai our souls. These wires constricted our development and thereby shaped us into something we aren't. Ultimately they cut us off from our true-self. In the beginning, we saw these wires as crucial to our success. We thought of them as leading the way to personal glory. They were shaping us to become perfect. But at some point they started to cut into our flesh, into our soul, twisting us and forcing us to grow in warped directions. We thought we were growing into our most beautiful self, but the directions were faulty. We came to a point where we weren't even certain of who we really were. Our true-self, which longed to break free of the constraints, was lost in the twisted perfect self we thought we were creating.

From a psychological perspective, our natural urge is to drive or grow toward self-realization, but we redirected the energy of that urge into making ourselves look like our idealized image (Horney 1950). Recovery showed us a way to release the constrictions of our idealized-self—that is, to loosen the bonds of the wires we had warped our soul with. It helped us redirect the energies of self-actualization back to our real-self. Recovery helped us release our true-self.

Even though we have made much progress, sometimes we fool ourselves into thinking we have completely let go of our false-self and its ideals. We haven't. It's like we take the so-called dirty shoe off one foot, our false-self, and put it on the other, our recovery-self. A dirty shoe is still a dirty shoe. It's not any cleaner because it is put on the foot of recovery.

Let me clarify what is happening here. Our thinking goes something like this: "Now that I possess the powerful principles of the Twelve Steps, I can finally make myself perfect." We mistake the gift of recovery for a tool to sculpt our idealized-self. Now we will master the art of bonsai! Finally, we can become perfect. We can be that person we think we need to be in order to be loved.

But achieving perfection isn't any more of a possibility in recovery than it was before. Quite the opposite.

Embracing Imperfection

So the first idea we need to accept if we are going to develop a healthy perspective toward ourselves is that we will never, and I mean *never*, be able to achieve perfection. To achieve emotional sobriety we need to *let go of our old ideas* because any life solution based on an alienation from our true-self will never work. Our goal should not be perfection. In fact, as you will see, our best goal is to embrace our imperfections so we can gain a healthy perspective on who we are in real life and work toward becoming our true-self. Still, the siren call of perfection beckons us. Someone once said that it's okay to strive for perfection if we never fool ourselves into believing we can achieve it. There may be some value in this perspective, but I have found that viewpoint dangerous—for me. That's because a part of me still hears in it the possibility that I can be perfect—that I can warp myself into that idealized-self. You may hear the call too, as one of the things we suffer from is this sense of uniqueness. In recovery it's often referred to as "terminal uniqueness" because this irrational belief can eventually lead us back to addiction, with terminal consequences. Part of me still believes that while most people can never achieve perfection, I am somehow different. I can be perfect. Maybe you can't, but I can.

What nonsense. For me it's safer to remind myself to "strive for progress, not perfection." This way I won't be confused.

Hopefully you are realizing that we cannot solve our problems with the thinking or the strategy that caused them in the first place. Striving to be perfect, to be someone we are not, will never work. Never! It just doesn't make sense, does it? So we need to shift our thinking, which means we need to develop a new perspective toward ourselves, toward life, toward our use of alcohol and other drugs, toward our relationships, toward our concept of responsibility, toward our feelings, toward our concept of spirituality, and toward our personal issues. That perspective must include the acceptance that perfection is a tragic myth—one that threatens to bury our true-self.

Our strategy must be to replace the siren call of perfection with a healthy perspective on our own true-self, warts and all. What a paradox—that when we quit trying to be our perfect, idealized-self and instead embrace the imperfections of our true nature, we might actually make progress!

But in recovery we learn the power of paradox. And one important paradox is that our wounds let grace and spirituality enter our lives. In recovery, our weaknesses become strengths. Admitting our powerlessness helps us find a better source of strength. Embracing our imperfections helps us find our true-self. And surprisingly, that true-self may prove to be better, much better, than the idealized one we were trying to perfect.

A Spirituality of Imperfection

Bill Wilson is quoted as saying, "Recovery is dependent upon a spiritual experience that is set on a pedestal of hopelessness" (Mooney 2010). It is quite paradoxical that something as wonderful as recovery grows out of something so dark and foreboding as helplessness or hopelessness. Hopelessness, however, becomes the catalyst for recovery.

Recovery transforms our wounds into something sacred. It's like a spiritual alchemy that transforms lead into gold. This is achieved through self-acceptance. Dr. Nathaniel Branden, a pioneer in the field of self-esteem, defined it this way:

> To be self-accepting is to be on my side—to be for me . . .
> Self-acceptance entails our willingness to experience—
> that is, to make real to ourselves, without denial or
> evasion—that we think what we think, feel what we

feel, desire what we desire, have done what we have done, and are what we are. It is the refusal to regard any part of ourselves—our bodies, our emotions, our thoughts, our actions, our dreams—as alien, as not me. (1994, 91)

When we accept ourselves as we are, as addicts, imperfect and unworthy, and surrender to the process of recovery and do the work—the real, tough work—our wound becomes a sacred wound. We've turned a weakness into a strength. Bill Wilson's sacred wound, his recovery from alcoholism, allowed him to help Dr. Bob. It is our sacred wound that allows us to help others who are suffering from addiction.

Ernest Kurtz, in his wonderful book *The Spirituality of Imperfection*, noted that "Spirituality has to do with the reality of the here and now, with living humanly as one is, with the very real, very agonizing, passions of the soul. Spirituality involves learning how to live with imperfection" (1993, 18).

This is a very different way of thinking about spirituality, isn't it? The religion I was exposed to as a child seemed to be based on a spirituality of perfection. I remember always feeling like I would never be able to live up to their standards. And from my limited perspective, it didn't seem like anyone else was either, despite their claims. The impossible is impossible. Perfection is humanly impossible.

When I found my way home in Twelve Step recovery, I found a spirituality based on imperfection, not perfection. This fit. I could relate to it because I had come to the point where I no longer could run and hide from my addiction and imperfections.

Getting Started on Self-Acceptance

So accepting and finally embracing our imperfections helps us keep a hold of ourselves and our humility when we fall short, when we make a mistake, when we have a lapse in our program or judgment, when we experience failure, or when we do something stupid. Self-acceptance helps us witness our own imperfections without collapsing into self-recrimination or self-hate. Humility allows us to feel some sympathy for our suffering, which is necessary before we set ourselves on a more constructive path.

I encourage couples I see in my practice to use the phrase "*of course we are having a problem*" whenever they encounter a tough patch in their relationship. This helps right-size the problem instead of *awfulizing* it. This phrase was designed to help couples hold on to a healthier perspective of their issues. This same concept may be useful in dealing with ourselves too.

Learn to say to yourself, "*Of course* I made a mistake, or had a lapse in my program, or experienced a failure, or did something stupid. I am imperfect and it's not a crime. I made a mistake, but I am not a mistake."

I often say to my clients, "*Get off your back and on your side.*"

Now please don't misunderstand me. I am not advocating an abdication of personal responsibility. Quite the opposite. When I suggest that we embrace our imperfection, I do not mean that everything we do is okay. It's not. But by moving beyond self-recrimination and self-loathing, we can learn from our experiences. Learning comes when we support ourselves, not when we condemn or criticize ourselves.

But there's a danger with this approach too. If we use the "of course" to *justify* rotten behavior, we are really playing a dirty trick on ourselves and on others too. This tool is to help us learn from our mistakes, not to justify them or avoid taking responsibility for them. In actual practice, accepting ourselves as we are does not encourage undesired behavior, but reduces the likelihood of it recurring.

Respect Feelings but Don't Give Them Privilege

So we can embrace our imperfections as a way to release the wires our idealized-self has wrapped around our true-self. Another thing that will help us get a better hold of ourselves is to critically evaluate our relationship with our feelings. How do we relate to what we feel? How aware are we of our feelings and how they manifest themselves in our lives? Are we aware when we feel anxious or threatened? Do we treat our feelings like they are a friend or an enemy? Do we hide what we feel or disown our feelings? Are we able to express what we feel, or does it take an act of Congress to get us to talk about what is going on? Do we give our feelings too much authority and privilege? Do we respect our feelings?

Having a healthy relationship with our feelings is critical to self-differentiation and growing up emotionally. The question is, What would a healthy relationship with our feelings look like? How would we relate to what we are feeling, and how would we respond to our feelings?

The first thing we need to realize is that it is healthy to embrace all that we feel. This doesn't mean we *act* on all of our feelings, because that wouldn't be healthy. It merely means that we acknowledge and accept what we are feeling—that we are open to our experience and open to use our feelings to learn more about ourselves.

Healthy people are aware of their feelings and accept them, including the ones that society or the false-self disallows. "Sometimes I am sensitive, and at other times I am insensitive. Sometimes I am easygoing, and at other times I am not. Sometimes I am soft and caring, and other times when I feel threatened, I am hard and protective. Sometimes I am humble and open; sometimes I am arrogant and closed."

This doesn't mean that healthy individuals don't have any blind spots, because they do. The point is that healthy people are willing to acknowledge a new notion of themselves (a notion of imperfection) and incorporate that into their self-concept.

People who are undifferentiated suffer from massive holes in their awareness. Unhealthy people are rigid and have a stereotyped image of themselves and how they are supposed to act and feel. Therefore they are unable to accept many parts of themselves and their feelings. They reject their true-self and force themselves to fit their idealized image.

It's also important to realize that feelings are not an infallible guide to the truth. Now, this may go against what you have been told. It is common to hear "trust your feelings" from a therapist or in a Twelve Step meeting. I believe it's important to *respect* our feelings. No question about it. But we create problems when we give our feelings too much privilege in our lives.

In previous chapters, we have discussed how emotional dependency distorts our perceptions. The gravitational force of emotional fusion sucks us toward a state in which we take things personally— as in, I feel threatened and anxious that you won't accept me or like me, or that we won't be close, or that we are too close.

Let's take a specific example in which giving feelings privilege feeds into the gravitational force of emotional dependency. Perhaps my supervisor was short with me when she was giving me instructions. The less differentiated I am, the more likely I will take her behavior personally and feel hurt, imagining that she doesn't like me or respect me. I *awfulize* the reasons behind her behavior. If I investigated the situation before reacting and drawing the wrong conclusion, I might discover that she was curt with me because she was overwhelmed. Her behavior had nothing to do with me. The so-called Imperial Self strikes again.

Because our feelings can be distorted by our personal issues, we need to *check things out* before jumping to conclusions. We are warned about the problems that having "contempt prior to investigation" can cause in relationships. You see, it is easy to draw the wrong conclusions from feelings influenced by anxiety. We need to check things out by asking, *"It seems like you are upset with me; is this true?"* Such a simple inquiry can go a long way toward sorting things out and keeping us from *awfulizing.* Then our responses can be more thoughtful and anchored in reality rather than a reaction to our anxiety.

What would it look like if we respected our anxiety but did not give it privilege? The first thing we would do is not treat our feelings as an infallible guide to the truth. We'd check out our feelings to see if they are based on reality or imagined. We'd also stop empowering our anxiety.

I want to share a personal experience from my son's life—a young man who has had to work hard to strip anxiety of its power. He has given me permission to relate this to you in hope that it will help someone else.

My son, Nicolas, suffered from severe anxiety as a child. He was about ten years old when he began to exhibit symptoms consistent with obsessive-compulsive disorder (OCD). This disorder is characterized by obsessive thoughts and compulsive rituals. People suffering from this condition feel driven to perform certain rituals to contain their anxiety. One of Nicolas's rituals was to avoid stepping on cracks. But he had other rituals too. He loved playing soccer and he was pretty good at it. However, he would have to end every touch of the soccer ball with his right foot. He would also have to count to four before he could kick the soccer ball. His mother became aware of these issues, could see that they were beginning to interfere with his life, and decided he needed help. She talked it over with him and he agreed to see a therapist.

Nicolas was remarkably honest with the therapist and described in rich detail the several rituals he felt compelled to perform. When he was finished, the therapist asked him a very powerful question: "What would happen if you didn't do one of your rituals?" Nicolas stopped and pondered this question for several seconds and then thoughtfully replied, "I would feel uncomfortable." She asked him if he could live with feeling uncomfortable. She told him that she knew it would be hard but that no one would die, nothing catastrophic would happen, other than that he would feel uncomfortable. Feeling uncomfortable was unfortunate but couldn't be helped. Could this be okay? Nicolas really listened to what the therapist told him, and it significantly shifted his perspective, as you are about to see.

A couple of weeks ago we were on a hike, and I asked him how he was doing with his anxiety and whether he still felt compelled to perform certain rituals. He said that the therapy he had as a child was incredibly helpful. It helped him put his anxiety in perspective. What he realized was that he could live with the discomfort that would occur if he did not perform a ritual, which took away a lot of its power. Yes, he still had obsessive thoughts about performing the rituals and sometimes he did, but they didn't control him. He felt he now had a choice.

Nick's struggle with anxiety provides us with a wonderful example of what it means to respect our feelings but not give them privilege. He stopped giving his obsessive thoughts the authority to run his life. It certainly warmed my heart to hear how well he was doing.

So by accepting (but not privileging) our feelings, we can begin to sort them out. We can begin to discover what is real, what is imagined, and what feelings are based on erroneous perceptions driven by our emotional dependency. As we learn to listen to our feelings without privileging them, we will gain insight into the personal issues that lie beneath our tendency to take things personally and invest too much faith in our feelings. We'll also get some clues regarding what we need to do to address these personal issues.

Understanding Our Emotional Themes

Our psychological and emotional wounds leave scars that show up in our behavior. Remember, the psychological climate of our culture and the emotional climate of our family encouraged us to reject our true-self and develop an idealized image of who we should be. No one is immune to this process. Our anxiety hijacked the energy intended for self-actualization and used it to create the false-self that corresponded to our idealized image. This false-self organized around one of three different *emotional themes*: (1) to rebel against, dominate, or scapegoat others; (2) to submit ourselves to the wishes, demands, or needs of others; or (3) to run away and emotionally withdraw. Earlier we discussed these as *moving against, moving toward*, and *moving away*. Our reaction to stress and anxiety can take any one of these paths. They are all possibilities, but one will be dominant. It's like being right handed. It doesn't mean we don't use our left hand; it's just that we have a preference for our right hand.

Our dominant way of dealing with stress and anxiety creates an emotional theme in our lives. We either move against people, move toward them, or move away from them. Learning which pattern we follow most often reveals how we answered the question, "Who should we be to have love and acceptance?"

In "Smart Thing 1," I suggested an exercise in which you took an emotional inventory. One benefit of this exercise is to help you gain some insight into the nature of your reactions. (Remember, the exercise had you describe an upsetting event; in column 4 of the table, you described how you reacted.) Your most usual reaction to an upsetting event is the "emotional theme" around which your idealized-self has organized itself. By revisiting this chart, you can begin to see which emotional theme is dominant for you—moving against, moving toward, or moving away.

If you haven't done the exercise yet, this might be a good time to return to that chapter and do so. If you have been able to identify your emotional theme, that's great; if you haven't, then what I am going to say still applies and may be integrated more specifically later.

Many of us identify with our idealized-self. If we don't, we identify with our *despised-self.* Our despised-self is composed of any part of us that is other than the idealized-self. So we are both of these things, but we are also much more than the sum of these two parts. We are also our *possible* self, our true-self. While we may have rejected our true-self, it is still there, bound by the wires of the false-self. It lives within us and has been knocking on the door of our spirits for a long time. This is what Dr. Jung meant when he wrote to Bill Wilson that alcoholism was a sign of a spiritual thirst.

This speaks to the heart of what I mean when I tell my patients that it is not what is wrong with you that's the problem. Rather, it's what's right about you that creates the problems in your life. There's a part of you, your real-self, that is dying to be expressed. It wants you to allow it to have more of a voice in your life. This part of you wants you to become your best self, your possible self. It wants you to cut the wires you used when you bonsai'd your soul. It wants to be set free.

This basic need for you to become your true-self is incredibly powerful. Dr. Abraham Maslow (1962) noted that something must be considered a basic need if it meets the following conditions: (1) its absence breeds illness, (2) its presence prevents illness, and (3) its restoration cures illness. This is a remarkably accurate description of what happens with our true-self. When we lose our true-self, we become ill, spiritually sick. This makes us vulnerable to addictions and psychiatric illness. If we hold on to ourselves, we stay balanced and healthy, and when we recover our lost true-self, we get well. This doesn't mean we will be cured of our addiction, because there is no cure. But through our recovery we learn to manage our malady one day at a time for the rest of our lives. This is true also of chronic psychiatric illnesses.

The bottom line is that we accept ourselves and make this self-acceptance the foundation of our lives. This is where we need to plant our center of gravity, right smack in the middle of who we are. This includes our imperfections, our feelings, our emotional themes, and our personal issues—everything.

Self-acceptance unlocks the door to our possible self. It helps us hold on to ourselves, especially when the going gets tough. Life is difficult, but even more so when we reject ourselves. When it's two against no one, we don't have a chance.

Accepting ourselves is extremely important to holding on to ourselves. Learning how to accept what happens in our relationships is important too. In the next chapter we will focus on how to see beyond the expectations generated by our emotional dependency.

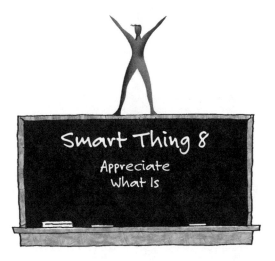

Smart Thing 8
Appreciate What Is

Perception is influenced by our state of mind. Here's a great example. For a class assignment in research methods in psychology, we had to record the different types of graffiti on the bathroom walls of the various departments at California State University, Long Beach. In the men's restroom in the psychology department, I found the following inscription: "Reality is for people who can't handle drugs." Clearly this was written by an addict whose twisted perceptions glorified drug use. I could relate. Because of my addiction, I twisted and distorted reality to support my continued use of alcohol and other drugs. My recovery started when I became honest with myself and saw my life for what it was, not what I wanted it to be. Seeing *what is true* is critical to being able to cope with life.

Addiction isn't the only thing that causes a distortion of reality. Emotional dependency influences and distorts our perception too. Seeing *what is* is nearly impossible with the filter that our emotional dependency places on our senses. It's like looking at life through a kaleidoscope. What is—reality—is twisted and distorted. Sometimes it is impossible even to make sense out of what we are looking at through the eyepiece. The more differentiated we are, the less distorted our field of vision. The less differentiated we are, the more powerful the kaleidoscope.

Distortion prevents us from achieving emotional sobriety because we need to acknowledge and appreciate *what is* in order to hold on to ourselves. Let's look at the havoc being poorly differentiated—failing to see and *appreciate what is*—causes in our lives.

According to Dr. John Gottman, renowned researcher on marital stability, turning toward your partner for what you need is an important characteristic of a healthy relationship. If you are lonely and you want to be closer to your partner, turning toward that person and expressing what you want is important. If you are hurt and in need of comfort, it's good to let your partner know. But what happens when your partner is not interested? What happens when that person is unavailable to meet your needs? The more emotionally fused we are, the more difficulty this will create.

When they came to see me, Jim and Sue had been married for six years. They were one of those program romance stories we have all heard about. They met at the Sunday morning beach meeting, and after a year of friendship, their sponsors gave them the green light to start dating. They were really excited about meeting each other. They both wanted a partner who would accept their recovery and understand the importance of working a program. They found this acceptance and understanding in each other. What they weren't prepared for were the challenges that they would face in the near future. The truth is we are never prepared for what happens in life. Yes, the fact that they both worked a strong Twelve Step program was beneficial, but it didn't prepare them for dealing with this crisis. You see, they hadn't worked on their emotional sobriety, and this became painfully evident during their fifth year of marriage.

Jim had never been married before, but this was Sue's second marriage. She had one child with her first husband. Jordan was a beautiful child with an amazing spirit. She was a joy to be around. She was the apple of Sue's eye, and Jim had grown very attached to her too.

Sue's first husband died in an unfortunate accident in the harbor of San Pedro, California. He was crushed when a crane operator lost control of a container that was being loaded into the hold of a ship. This catastrophe inspired Sue to get help for her drinking. Jordan was one year old when her father was killed. Sue met Jim when Jordan was two and a half.

Jim loved playing with Jordan—this is one of the things that attracted Sue to Jim. He was wonderful with Jordan and became very attached to her. After Jim and Sue married, Jim became Jordan's father, psychologically and emotionally, and he adopted her. They were as deeply bonded as Sue and Jordan.

Jordan suddenly fell ill with a very bizarre set of life-threatening symptoms, and Jim and Sue became incredibly anxious, as any parent would have. The next six months were spent bouncing between doctors in hopes that someone could identify what was wrong with Jordan and help her. Sensing that she was dying, she started talking with her mother and father about what would happen when she died. Where would her body go, where would her spirit go? Will I see you again? I'm certain that I don't need to tell you how terribly painful this conversation must have been. Words cannot capture what Jim and Sue must have felt during these conversations.

When they described this to me, I listened with tears rolling down my cheeks. Their pain and suffering was devastating and shattered all my defenses. For a year and a half they had witnessed the decline in Jordan's health. They watched her beautiful spirit grow dimmer and dimmer. They watched her die. Watching your child die is devastating. Feeling so helpless and powerless when you see that your child is in this kind of danger must be unbearable.

Jim and Sue were drained, depressed, angry, and outraged, and then when Jordan died, the next crisis in their lives started. They desperately needed comforting, soothing, something to help them bear the unbearable. Their lives were changed forever and not in a good way. Now whenever they looked at children, they both wondered what kind of unknown disease might be lurking in the child's DNA, ready to unleash its suffering on that child. The world was no longer a safe place. They felt betrayed. Life and even God had forsaken them. They thought they had each other, but after a while they were no longer even sure of that. They were constantly fighting or withdrawing from each other. It seemed as if they had lost each other along the way too. Their dreams and lives had shattered.

Jim and Sue had come to me hoping I could perform a miracle, but I told them that I wasn't a miracle worker, only a psychotherapist. There was no easy way to restore their connection.

Here is what was happening between Jim and Sue. They would come home from work feeling empty, grieving, lost, and sad and would turn to each other for comfort, but found none. Instead they'd receive anger, bitterness, blame, hurtful comments, or a deadly silence. They had nothing to give each other. They were spent, like empty shells. And yet their emotional dependency still found enough energy to express its demands. "Shoulds" started to fly. Sue would complain, "You should be more supportive of me. If you loved me, you would quit thinking about yourself and comfort me. She wasn't your biological daughter; she was mine. Can't you understand how I feel?"

Jim had his moments too: "You are so selfish; you have always been selfish; that's still your biggest problem. Why don't you work your program? Get out of yourself and help me. I need you right now!"

They were both in a terrible amount of pain. When we are stressed to this degree, our functional level of differentiation usually drops. Sue and Jim were taking everything personally. They were completely fused with each other. They had become emotional conjoined twins.

It is times like these my faith in the human potential becomes crucial to the process of therapy. I believe that if we go into the depths of our pain and suffering and stay there, eventually we will repair ourselves. Not only did Jim and Sue lose their daughter to a horrible disease, they lost themselves and each other as well.

But Jim and Sue needed more than my faith in the human spirit to deal with the crisis between them; they needed help in raising their differentiation. They needed to learn how to soothe and repair themselves instead of demanding to be comforted. Neither of them could take a hold of my faith in them until they got a better hold of themselves.

Their emotional dependency was impairing their ability to stay together during this crisis. To reduce this influence, I had to help them see beyond their limited horizon. They needed healthier ways of coping with their stress. Moving away from each other or against each other was exacerbating the problem and pushed them further apart. They both knew that attacking each other was self-defeating and destructive, but it seemed as if it was the only option. If all you have is a hammer in your tool box, then you start to treat everything like a nail. In reality, they were re-creating the emotional climate of their childhoods.

They wanted to find a safe harbor in each other, but all they found when they turned to each other was pain, anger, and resentment. They couldn't see each other. They were blinded by what their emotional dependency demanded.

The first thing I pointed out to them was that they were in the same room, but in different corners. They were both feeling a tremendous amount of grief and sadness, and neither one of them was skilled at comforting themselves. This is why they demanded comfort from each other. They had none to give themselves. No one in their families had ever helped them learn how to soothe themselves and repair themselves. When someone was hurt in their families, they attacked each other in order to feel close. This was how they acted to create togetherness. But it's a strange way of creating intimacy, isn't it? Needless to say, this wasn't a very effective coping strategy.

In order to learn how to hold on to themselves, the couple needed to first see what they were doing. They needed to realize that their attempts to solve the problem were only making it worse. Their fighting was their way of being together, of trying to feel connected, but it didn't work. It left them empty, bitter, and alone. As I pointed out to them, we usually have positive intentions, even in our worst behaviors. You see, they were trying to connect with each other; they just didn't know how to connect in a more effective manner.

Because their vision was impaired by their emotional fusion, they couldn't see what they had to offer each other. They only knew they were not receiving comfort, which obscured their desire for connection. It's almost like their desire to be connected and to comfort each other didn't matter, since it wasn't what they expected. I pointed out that they were connecting by moving against each other and that this wasn't very nurturing—in fact, it was often quite abusive. Even so, a desire for togetherness was evident. As I pointed this out to them, they both became quite thoughtful.

They knew they loved each other, and this knowledge made their difficulty connecting during this crisis even more baffling. I told them that instead of letting their emotional dependency construct the reality of their connection, they needed to let a different part of themselves have more say in the matter. I asked what part of them was hearing and recognizing what I was pointing out. This, I explained, was the part of them that may be helpful now. This part needed to be brought into the foreground of their lives.

I soon saw a shift in Jim and Sue; they were beginning to get a hold of themselves. They were not quite as lost in all of their suffering and in the real and perceived injustice and unfairness of their situation. Because of this, they started to *appreciate what they did have in their relationship.* They seemed comforted by the idea that they were connected, albeit in a negative way. While they didn't know how to soothe each other, they had something else: a shared desire to connect and a mutual ignorance of how to soothe themselves. This wasn't what they demanded or expected from each other, but in the long run it was much better. Relationships are people growers, especially when two people who love each other face the kind of gauntlet that Jim and Sue experienced.

All relationships—all of human life—is tinged by disappointment and frustration. Jim and Sue faced devastating events, perhaps among the most tragic that any person can experience. But Jim and Sue eventually found themselves—individually and as a couple—by virtue of accepting their disappointment, their loss, their devastation, and their mutual inability to soothe themselves as individuals or as a couple. And in that, they came face-to-face with a freeing reality of life: We gain emotional sobriety as we *learn to appreciate what is.* What Jim and Sue have to teach us is that the health of a relationship is determined by how we handle disappointment and frustration. For them, part of *appreciating what is* meant discovering the kernel of value in their mutual devastation—their opportunity to build something stronger than before. Though this will never replace the terrible loss of Jordan, it nevertheless *is what is* for Jim and Sue.

Whether or not we are in an intimate relationship, it is certain that we will experience hardships. The things we struggle with help us uncover *what is* in life. If we stay connected during this struggle—connected to ourselves, to each other, to our friends, to our recovery program—and do our best to keep a hold of ourselves, we will be able to discover and appreciate what is present, rather than feel upset and frustrated by what is not present.

Here's one final example. Again, it is a very difficult story, but one that reveals the strength to be gained in appreciating what is.

I worked with a family who lost their twenty-one-year-old son to a drug overdose. The family was angry: angry with the drug dealer who sold their son the heroin; angry with themselves for not being better parents; angry with their son for using drugs; angry with me for not helping their son; and angry with the disease for killing their son. They kept insisting that there was nothing to appreciate in their tragedy, but during one session I raised the idea that perhaps they could find something to appreciate about this time in their lives. This suggestion of finding something to appreciate that would help them deal with their grief was simply ridiculous to them. The following week they came in with a very different attitude. They were still grieving, but the anger had dissipated. I asked them what had happened. The father turned to me and said, "I really thought you were crazy after the advice you gave us in the last session. There was nothing to appreciate in our grief. And then I had an epiphany. I had twenty-one years with my son. He was in our lives for twenty-one years. If God had come to me and said, 'I will let you have a son but you can only have him for twenty-one years,' I would have gladly accepted God's conditions.

"I still wonder if you're crazy, Dr. Berger, but I have found something I can appreciate in my loss, that I had twenty-one years with my son and I am very grateful for each and every one of those years."

Emotional sobriety requires that we learn how to deal with what life expects from us, rather than insisting that life conform to our claims and expectations. Being fully present in the moment and seeing and *appreciating what is* rather than focusing on what is not can help us differentiate and integrate the most painful and challenging experiences in life, as these two tragic examples illustrate.

I chose these difficult stories because I wanted you to see that even in the worst situations we can find a perspective to help us hold on to ourselves, that there is still hope. We just need to trust the process and look beyond our emotional dependency for the solution. When we learn to *appreciate what is* in life, we will be on the path of emotional sobriety.

Now is a good time to focus on the healthy ways to comfort ourselves, which we'll do in the next chapter.

Smart Thing 9
Comfort Yourself When You Are Hurt or Disappointed

As we've seen, when we learn how to hold on to ourselves, we move our emotional sobriety forward. And holding on to ourselves means learning to care for ourselves and our self-esteem rather than depending on others to take care of us.

Another way of understanding this process is to think about it as *maintaining a relationship with ourselves.* By this, I mean that we need to think of ourselves as someone to be loved, cherished, respected, and cared for—someone who deserves the same attention we would devote to an intimate partner.

Just as we often unfairly dump on our intimate partners, so we unfairly dump on ourselves. Earlier I said that we save our worst behavior for those we love and care about, but that is only a partial truth. The greater truth is that we often treat ourselves far worse than we treat anyone else. We react to hurt or disappointment by criticizing ourselves, hating our vulnerability, and abandoning ourselves—things we'd never do to our best friend! If we seek emotional sobriety, we can no longer tolerate these self-destructive habits. We can no longer let emotional fusion make us dependent on others for soothing.

Learning to comfort ourselves and stand on our own two feet doesn't mean that we become an island of self-sufficiency and therefore don't need connection or togetherness. Connection is a basic need, like food or water. It's wonderful to be comforted by someone who cares about us. But we also need to be prepared to comfort ourselves when our partner or friend is emotionally or physically unavailable.

The capacity to comfort ourselves and maintain a relationship with ourselves when we are disappointed or wounded is the "acid test" of emotional sobriety. As it turns out, our difficulty is partly biological—it is related to how our brains function.

After an extensive comparison of the brains of reptiles, lower mammals, and higher mammals, neurologist Paul MacLean (1978) concluded that although the human brain has evolved in incredible ways and has expanded to a great size, it has retained some of the basic features of its ancestral relationship to reptiles, early mammals, and recent mammals. This makes it possible to identify three formations in the human brain that are radically different in their structure and function. This model is called the *triune* human brain.

Triune means "three." Our brains consist of three parts. The first part is called the reptilian brain (R-complex), the second is the mammalian brain (limbic system), and the third is the neocortex or cerebral cortex. This is the human brain. Let's discuss each of these areas and their functions.

- **Reptilian Brain:** This is the most primitive part of our brain, responsible for regulating basic functions such as breathing, digestion, and excretion. In addition, the reptilian brain is the source of imitative behaviors, a predisposition to routine and ritual, what researchers call *displacement behaviors*—inappropriate behaviors for a given situation when we are under stress (like smiling when we are anxious or frightened)—and *deceptive behaviors* (like conning some-one by creating false impressions).

This part of the brain is more automatic, reflexive, and instinctually driven, but it is poorly equipped to learn to cope or deal with new or novel situations. When we are stressed, we shift into survival mode and become highly reactive—relying more on our reptilian brain. When governed by these processes, our responses will be rigid and we will rely on rules, routines, or rituals to cope. In essence, stress compromises our ability to adapt and solve problems.

- **Mammalian Brain:** But survival is also mediated by the next part of the brain—the mammalian brain. This part of our brain involves the limbic system and the amygdala. The complex limbic system mediates such things as feed-ing, fighting, self-protective functions, procreation, sexual arousal, affectionate behaviors, nursing, emotional bonding, and maternal behaviors. It also mediates the expression and experience of emotions. Feelings ranging from fear to ecstasy to feelings of conviction are generated by this part of the brain.

  When this part of the brain is overly activated, we can become overwhelmed with feelings and easily lose sight of the bigger picture. Keeping sight of the bigger picture is the job of the next part of our brain.

- **Neocortex:** The neocortex is the part of the brain designed to find new solutions to challenges posed by the external world. This part of our brain created language and the associ-ated functions of reading, writing, and mathematics. It is the mother of invention and the father of abstract thought.

  The most recently evolved portion of the neocortex is the prefrontal cortex. This is the part of the brain that is contemplative and introspective. It allows us to look inward at our subjective experience. The prefrontal cortex is also responsible for planning, forethought, and foresight.

There is a complex relationship between these three parts of the brain. Our entire brain may be involved in any activity, but certain parts of the brain seem to be more activated than others. The part of our brain that is engaged depends on a complex interaction of how we appraise a situation, the values we place on the issues involved, and many other factors. Think about it this way: a certain part of our brain will always be the dominant force, and that part will determine the nature, intensity, and quality of our emotional and behavioral response.

Under most stressful circumstances, we want our neocortex running the show because it possesses the greatest adaptive sophistication and variability. However, when we feel threatened or anxious or have enough interpersonal pressure, survival reactions hardwired into the reptilian and mammalian parts of our brain take control. Our anxiety or pain increases our impulse to fight (or control), to submit, or to run away. Generally speaking, the part of your brain in control determines the behavior and emotions you display. When we are anxious or in pain, we typically behave like a reptile—we rely on routine and rigid ritual to solve problems.

Don't conclude that we are destined to react like reptiles anytime we're upset. However, understanding the strong pull to react this way can help you hold on to yourself—that is, help you put the neocortex back in the driver's seat. There are many things you can do to soothe yourself so that you don't have to fight, submit, or run away. You can maintain a sense of yourself and a relationship with yourself regardless of the situation or circumstance.

A psychological technique called neurolinguistic programming gives us ways to put the neocortex back in control. It teaches that we can change how we feel by doing any one of the following three things: (1) change our *focus*, (2) change our *language* (what we are saying to ourselves), or (3) change our *physiology*. Let's explore each of these in regard to soothing ourselves.

Changing Our Focus

If we expected to be comforted by the person who has disappointed or hurt us and they don't, we are stuck. We can't always change what someone is or isn't doing. Even though we know this truth, it doesn't seem to thwart us from trying. When we attempt to control those things that are not in our control, we become more stressed—more rigid and reptilian. We make the situation worse. To regain our capacity to comfort ourselves, we have to change focus.

So the question is, *how do we change our focus?* We need to focus on something that can help us calm down and feel safe. One way to do this is to ask ourselves, "If a hurt or disappointed child approached, how would you comfort them? What would you say and do?"

Let's look at an example of how one of my clients learned to change focus.

Hector is a very successful attorney and a rather handsome man. At age forty-five, he has been married and divorced twice. When he came to see me, he had been divorced for almost three years and was actively dating for the past year and a half. He really fell for the most recent woman he had dated, Suzy.

He had known this woman for ten years. They lived on the same block. Their sons attended the same school. She was divorced too. Suzy was stunningly beautiful. Initially, she really seemed to care for him and value their relationship. He recalled comments she made about how she would love to reorganize his kitchen and make his home more comfortable. "It needs a woman's touch," she would say. He loved hearing these things. She also shared with him her fantasies of raising their children together. They both loved cats and long walks down at the beach. The relationship seemed to be going swimmingly.

Yet some things didn't feel right about their connection. Certain comments made Hector think that Suzy wanted someone to take care of her and that he was merely the next candidate for the job. He didn't like how she seemed to let her son get away with murder. He had some doubts about their compatibility, but he didn't discuss them with her or anyone, for that matter. He swallowed his feelings. He denied them.

But feelings will inevitably find a way to deliver their message to us. His feelings manifested themselves in the following ways. First, he often felt anxious, like he had to perform or behave a certain way when around her. He was always afraid that she would judge him (though this was most likely a projection of how *he* was judging her). Second, his doubt showed up in their sexual relationship. Sometimes he had trouble getting and maintaining an erection, and other times he had trouble having an orgasm when they made love. He attributed his sexual difficulties to the stress he was feeling at work.

Despite these denied feelings, Suzy became too important to him, too quickly. He was becoming more and more lost in their relationship. His way of responding to the increasing emotional dependency was by moving toward her, emotionally fusing with her. He tried harder and harder to please her and satisfy her every need. But this was too much togetherness for her, and she started distancing herself from him, which made him even more anxious. Finally, she ended the relationship, telling him they weren't sexually compatible. He was devastated, his pride shattered. He felt terribly inadequate and insecure.

He came to counseling because he was in a vicious, monthlong tailspin. He was anxious, depressed, sleepless, had lost fifteen pounds, and couldn't concentrate at work. He obsessed about Suzy and the relationship all the time. At times he experienced panic attacks, cried uncontrollably, or became angry with her for rejecting him.

As he described his loss and his shattered dreams, I empathized with his pain and told him that I could see that he was distraught. I let him know that he wasn't alone. I would be there with him and would walk through this experience with him and see if we could uncover and discover what made him so vulnerable. Though Hector did not realize it, his primitive brain was in complete control of his emotional reaction and reasoning. He needed to change focus to pull out of the tailspin.

To help him shift his focus, I started talking to him about slowing down and really taking in the things he didn't like about Suzy. I invited him to see what they meant for him and his hopes of having a loving and wonderful relationship. As he shifted focus, he revealed the doubts he'd had about the quality of the life that they would have shared if their relationship progressed and they married. There were deep differences in their attitudes about material things, their need to be part of high society, their values about parenting, and much more. As he stopped and really considered the implications of these differences, he was struck by *how well he could ignore issues that were so important.*

In one session, I suggested that the sexual difficulties he had may have been his body's way of speaking his mind. He asked me what I meant. I explained that he didn't seem to have sexual performance issues with anyone else. Maybe his body knew that she wasn't right for him, for whatever reason, but that he wouldn't stop and face how he really felt. I told him, "It doesn't seem like there is room for *you* in your relationships." This helped, but the next intervention helped even more.

I reframed the problem he was having. I told him that the problem wasn't Suzy's rejection; it was that he didn't take care of himself. He didn't protect himself. He didn't protect the little boy who wanted everyone to love him. He didn't honor his own desires, values, and needs. This touched something very deep and painful. He sobbed, his chest heaving. When he finally put words to his pain, he said that this had been the problem during his entire adult life. He never protected himself—not in his first marriage, his second, nor with Suzy.

He chose really attractive women who would make him feel good about himself but who had little of the substance he needed. They were concerned with their image and status, not who they were. These gorgeous women allowed him to increase his sense of personal value. *He borrowed his own self-esteem from their beauty*. But he ignored his feelings when he started to realize that he actually didn't like these women.

As we further explored this dynamic, he recalled how left out and awkward he felt as a child, especially during his teenage years. The girls didn't find him attractive. He was a late bloomer athletically and usually picked last for baseball or basketball games. He felt ugly, unlovable, inadequate, and insecure. His real or imagined perception was that his parents or friends weren't available to discuss these kind of feelings, so, like most of us, he suffered and struggled in silence.

Hector learned early in life to move toward people to please them as a way to resolve this pain. This was how he would be loved and accepted. But this strategy came at a terrible price—he had to abandon himself to pull it off. He now realized that this had to change if he was ever going to be happy and fulfilled.

I asked him to talk to the part of himself he abandoned. I put an empty chair in front of him, and he started a very important dialogue with the part of himself that he didn't like. Through this process, he began to understand this part of himself. He started to claim the part of himself that he had disowned, shifting his focus to developing a more robust, integrated sense of himself. He also comforted himself by addressing the hurt and disappointment he had experienced as a teenager. How Suzy had wronged him was no longer his focus; now he focused on himself. Soon his anxiety and depression disappeared, and he asked his psychiatrist to take him off all psychotropic medications. He gained weight, started sleeping better, and became more productive at work.

Hector soothed himself by embracing the part of himself that he had abandoned because of his false-self. He shifted the focus from being rejected (which was a threat, activating his reptilian brain) to how he came to abandon himself (which required his neocortex, his reasoning skills). He realized that he was hurt by Suzy's rejection because it validated a deep belief that he was unlovable. Her rejection just echoed his own rejection. *Once he shifted the focus onto this issue, he was able to soothe himself.* He was able to soothe himself because he now felt that he would protect himself from falling in love with the wrong person.

While I don't wish the kind of pain that Hector suffered on anyone, it is often true that it takes an emotional earthquake to open the door to healing. Fortunately, Hector chose to walk through the door.

Changing Our Language or Self-Talk

The way we talk to ourselves when we are hurt or disappointed will either help us soothe ourselves or make the situation worse. Thus, changing the way we talk to ourselves is a second line of defense against the tyranny of the reptilian brain. In the story above, Hector did more than change his focus about what happened in his relationship with Suzy. He also redefined the problem in a way that allowed him not only to maintain a relationship with himself, but to improve it. He changed the way he talked about the problem by talking to *himself* in a new way. (Remember, we even pulled up an empty chair so he could talk to himself.)

Initially, Hector thought he wasn't good enough for Suzy. Her rejection reinforced his worst fear. But the real problem was that Hector rejected himself and had abandoned himself long before he met Suzy!

In therapy, Hector turned toward himself and learned how to protect this little-boy self who desperately wanted love and acceptance. He learned how to maintain a relationship with himself, with *all* of himself. He brought his neocortex into play by talking to himself in a new way. His adult self took over and provided the protection for his little boy, who had indiscriminately sought the approval of Suzy and everyone else he came across. But his adult self could see the bigger picture because he was now using his neocortex.

When Hector turned against himself by thinking he wasn't good enough for Suzy, he fragmented himself and went into survival mode. When we are in conflict with ourselves, we will never be able to find comfort or be comforted. The only way we can comfort ourselves is by maintaining a positive relationship with ourselves.

We become devastated by someone else's rejection because it reactivates the anxiety that caused us to reject ourselves in the first place. In a way, their rejection starts a feedback loop that says we were right when we originally concluded that we couldn't be loved and accepted. But the truth is that rejection is a myth. *We have confused rejection with approval.* The part of our brain that reacts to rejection isn't thoughtful or reflective; it is reflexive.

When we step back and regain perspective, we can see that we are not a piece of meat to be stamped "USDA approved." If someone doesn't connect with us, they just don't connect with us! That's all it means. It's not because we are wrong; we are just wrong for them.

If you go into a restaurant and order a hamburger instead of a tuna sandwich, you are not rejecting the tuna sandwich. You simply have a preference for a hamburger at that time.

In fact, there is now some neurobiological evidence that says that through our sense of smell we can assess if a person is a good fit for us in terms of procreation. If my pheromones don't turn you on, they just don't turn you on. This is why we like some colognes and not others. We are all unique and have different needs and preferences. The fact that I don't fit the needs and preferences of one person doesn't mean I am no good or unworthy.

Dr. Fritz Perls reminded us about this when he said, "I am not in this world to live up to your expectations. And you are not in this world to live up to mine. If by chance we meet, fine. If not, it can't be helped" (1969, 4). This perspective helps us soothe ourselves when we are hurt by rejection.

The next time you are hurt and disappointed, check out what you are saying to yourself. If you are struggling and in a lot of pain, I can almost guarantee that your self-talk is making things worse. This means that the way you are talking to yourself about the situation is making it hard to soothe yourself. So dig into what you are doing.

If you are honest with yourself, you'll likely discover that you are taking the situation personally. If you are, then this exercise might help. Lean into the rejection and what you are saying to yourself. Take it to the extreme. Be as outrageous and absurd as possible. Set aside all reason. Here's an example.

If Hector had done this exercise, he would have probably said things like this:

- If I were a better man, Suzy would have fallen in love with me.
- Who I am determines what you will do and how you will feel toward me.

- I am so powerful that I can control your feelings.
- Suzy has the authority to say if I am okay or not.

Hopefully you can see the absurdity in these statements. (If not, I hope you'll take this chapter to heart and identify and reframe your own negative messages, as we do with Hector below.)

When we give ourselves permission to be absurd and outrageous, we see how extreme our usual reactions are and automatically move to a more balanced perspective. We are hardwired to move in this direction, but we can only repair ourselves when we become aware of what we are doing. Here's where Hector may have ended up if he did the previous exercise:

- Suzy and I are different and we want different things from a relationship.
- Suzy feels the way she does and I feel the way I do.
- I am responsible for myself and Suzy is responsible for herself.
- I don't need to be liked or approved of by Suzy to be okay.

If we face our loss or broken dreams without filtering them through self-hate, we will naturally grieve the loss. Grieving is healthy and necessary. It helps us integrate the loss and learn from the experience. But this process is interrupted when we turn against ourselves. Changing our physiology can help us comfort ourselves too.

Changing Our Physiology

Try smiling when you feel down. It's hard to stay depressed if you are smiling; it's hard to smile if you are depressed. Dr. Dan Siegel, a psychiatrist and author of *The Developing Mind*, hands his depressed patients a prescription that surprises them. He doesn't prescribe them an antidepressant medication. It's a prescription for aerobic exercise.

He asks his depressed patients to go out and exercise several times a week and then come back to see him in a month. If they follow his advice, they typically are less depressed at the next appointment.

We know that there is a complex and reciprocal mind-body relationship. Change the mind and the body will change; change the body and the mind will change. When I observe patients who are deeply disappointed or in pain, they often start to spontaneously sway back and forth. They are rocking themselves. They are unconsciously soothing themselves. They don't recognize what they are doing.

You see, we have many ideas about what we should and shouldn't do if we are adults. Rocking ourselves is considered okay for children but not for adults. Crying is considered more okay for children (depending on your family) than it is for adults. Being held is okay for a child who needs comfort but is not okay for an adult. The list of physiological options we deny ourselves is never-ending.

Unlike changing our focus and changing our self-talk, smiling, exercising, and crying happen in the real, physical world. And changing our physiology in real time is our third line of defense against the reptilian response. The truth is that anything you need to do to comfort yourself is okay as long as you don't become too self-indulgent or harm someone else. For example, you can give yourself permission to eat a comfort food as long as you don't overindulge (which would lead to more self-criticism and self-contempt). So eat one pint of Häagen-Dazs ice cream, not ten. Buy a rocking chair and put on some of your favorite music and rock. While you are in your car with the windows rolled up, scream, yell, curse, put words to your pain or disappointment. Go get a massage. *Change your physiology.*

A note on comforting others: There is one other approach to comforting ourselves that is recommended in recovery. It is often referred to as *getting out of yourself.* This approach is based on the St. Francis prayer that says, "It is better to comfort than to be comforted." This approach has its value too, *but only if we expand its scope to include ourselves*. Comforting others is a great way to deal with our pain, but some of us use it to avoid dealing with ourselves. I urge you not to hide behind this great tool. Try the others first.

Self-Comfort Is a Key to Emotional Sobriety

We need to learn how to comfort ourselves when we are hurt or disappointed in order to keep our autonomy in relationships. When we take responsibility for our own emotional soothing, we can freely give comfort or ask for comfort. Moreover, when we turn to someone and they are not available to comfort us, we can soothe ourselves. If we can take care of ourselves, we won't become resentful and demand their attention. We won't stake a claim to our right to be comforted by telling them, "If you loved me . . . " What a gift for both of us!

Our new skill brings many benefits. It creates room in our relationships for ourselves, our partner, our friends, and our families. People enjoy being with us, instead of fearing that they will disappoint us or let us down. We grow up emotionally and stand on our own two feet. We are closing in on emotional sobriety.

If none of the suggestions in this book help, then it may be time to seek professional help. You are stuck. This is where psychotherapy can be very useful in recovery. Find a therapist who can help you develop better ways to cope with your disappointment or pain. Interview several therapists and trust your instinct. I always tell potential patients that in our first session they will know if I can help them. Even though I am pretty good at what I do, if they are "allergic to me," then I am not good for them. Penicillin is a great drug and can help many people, but not if you are allergic to it—then it might kill you.

In the next chapter, I will discuss another important tool to help you hold on to yourself—the concept of a personal compass and how it can guide you through uncertainty and anxiety.

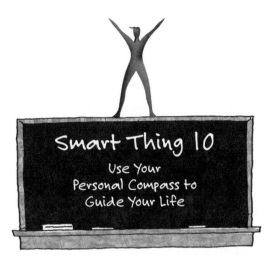

Smart Thing 10
Use Your Personal Compass to Guide Your Life

What do we do when we are lost? How do we find our way? What signs tell us we are heading in the right direction?

We've all raised these questions at one time or another. As it turns out, the answers to these questions are highly relevant to emotional sobriety. A personal compass that points to true north is an essential piece of equipment for our journey. Let me explain this idea further.

A personal compass guides our lives just like a real compass guides our direction when we are traveling. It tells us what direction to go when we are lost or uncertain. As any compass does, it points to true north. Knowing true north allows us to orient ourselves. It helps us determine where we are currently heading and how to get back on track when we are lost.

But the proper functioning of a real compass can be corrupted by magnetic fields other than the North Pole. If you place a magnet close to a compass, it will create a false true north. The arrow of the compass will point to the magnet. If you move the magnet around the compass, the compass needle will follow it, and you will not be able to determine any direction. In either case, when a compass is influenced by another strong magnetic field, it can no longer be trusted to guide us properly. A corrupted compass is misleading and confusing.

A similar problem can develop with our personal compass. It can become compromised by other powerful forces and therefore no longer point to our true north. Two forces that mess up our personal compass are (1) our false-self and (2) addiction.

The False-Self and Our Personal Compass

When we created an idealized image of who we should be, what we should do, and how we should feel, we lost our connection to our true-self. Our true north lost its meaning and became defined by our false-self. It no longer pointed to what our true-self wanted or desired, but rather pointed to a direction determined by our idealized-self.

Sal was a forty-five-year-old family practice medical doctor with a full-time practice. He was moderately to severely depressed when he came to see me. When we are depressed, it is typically hard to identify the cause of our depression. Depression creates a fog that interferes with cognitive functioning. Therefore it is usually unproductive to ask a depressed person the question, "What is making you depressed?" Often they will say, "I don't know." This is a genuine "I don't know." It is not an avoidance.

Sal didn't know the cause of his depression, but he knew it had been growing stronger over the past five years. As he described what he had been struggling with over this period of time, he said he was dissatisfied and not fulfilled with practicing medicine. He had always wanted to be a woodworker. He loved making furniture and he thought he was pretty good at it.

Sal recalled, however, that there was never a question about what he would do with his life. He became a doctor to please his father. His parents both immigrated to the United States from Italy. It was tough going for them. His father was a cellist. He loved playing the cello but had lots of trouble finding work. In order to survive, he eventually had to surrender his dream of playing in an orchestra and instead became a butcher. "What a pity," Sal remarked. "He worked long days and very hard to provide for us. But I don't believe he ever played the cello again."

Sal remembered his father telling him, "You will be a doctor, my son. You won't have to butcher meat like I do to make a living. I want you to have a better life." Sal was a very good student and studied hard. He went to medical school at UCLA and did a residency in family medicine. He liked helping people and interacting with them, he enjoyed the financial freedom that the practice of medicine had given him, but he was unhappy. He was upset with himself because he wasn't satisfied with the life he had. "Anyone would love my lifestyle," he said. He discounted his true feelings, yet he couldn't deny that something was still wrong.

He felt that he couldn't give up medicine to follow his dream of being a woodworker, especially after his father had sacrificed so much to help him become a doctor. "I would be ungrateful, wouldn't I?" he asked. "It would destroy my father," he said. He was conflicted and stuck between being a "good son" and honoring his wish to work with wood, to pursue his dream.

I put an empty chair in front of Sal and asked him to have a dialogue between these two parts of himself. He started this exercise by speaking from the side of himself that wanted to work with wood. He said, "I need a voice in your life. You are killing me by telling me that there is no room for me."

The "good son" responded, "I am obliged to practice medicine. I owe it to my father; what kind of a son would I be if I made his sacrifices meaningless?"

When he switched chairs and responded to the "good son," he said, "We would honor our father more if we didn't make his same mistake. He gave up his dream to play the cello and we are doing the same thing, and it's making me depressed."

A lightbulb lit up in Sal's consciousness. Yes, he was honoring his father's wish for him to be a doctor, but he was also ignoring his wish to work with wood just as his father had ignored his desire to play the cello. In the Old Testament, the Lord says to Moses, "The sins of the father will be passed along to the children" (Exodus 34:7). Though we are not speaking of sin here, the principle is much the same: we tend to repeat or relive our parents' condition in some way. In this case, Sal's father had turned away from his native love and talent to fulfill an important duty—the duty of caring for his family. Out of loyalty, Sal was reenacting the loss that his father had experienced. Oftentimes our loyalty to our parents is misguided.

Sal's personal compass pointed in the wrong direction because it was being overly influenced by his idealized-self. This false-self demanded that he give up what was important to him and please his father. He had to be the "good son"; there was no other option.

But this put Sal in a dilemma. His didn't see how he could give his creative side a voice without being disloyal to his father. Our true-self strives for wholeness. Sal's depression indicated he was not moving in the direction of wholeness but was suffering a kind of spiritual sickness that came from failing to integrate his creative self into his life. Out of loyalty to his father's wishes, Sal interrupted what he would have naturally done and allowed his false-self to disturb the true north of his personal compass. From his father he learned to ignore his creative side. *He learned it wasn't okay to fol-*

low his true north. But he never realized that this is what he was doing. He had a blind spot. When he had the epiphany, it restored his true north. Awareness in and of itself is therapeutic. It restores our natural functioning.

In subsequent sessions, Sal began working on integrating these two parts of himself. He found a way to honor them both. Remember— the truth will set you free *but only if you have the courage to live it.* Sal did have the courage. He sold his practice and accepted a part-time position at a medical clinic. He also opened a wood shop where he began to design and build furniture. He integrated these two parts of himself. His depression lifted, and six years later it has not returned.

Another wonderful benefit of Sal's work unfolded when he asked his father to join him in a therapy session. He told his father about his conflict, how he had become depressed, and what he was doing with his life now. His father listened quietly. With tears in his eyes, he told Sal, "Son, I am proud of you. I didn't know how to accomplish what you are doing in your life today. I lost an important part of myself when I became a butcher. I am glad that you realized you didn't have to do that." Sal cried too.

I turned to his father and said, "I saw a cello for sale at the music store the other day. It's never too late for you to start playing again." He smiled knowingly.

Addiction and Our Personal Compass

Addiction has a devastating effect on our personal compass too. It also hijacks our life force and overrides our true-self. It is like a juggernaut that crushes everything in its path.

I recall one patient, Briezzia, who was threatened with losing her children if she continued drinking. Although the maternal instinct is incredibly powerful, not even this force could override her compulsion to drink. She continued to drink, telling herself she would be more discreet and remain in control.

Think about her decision to keep drinking for a moment. *If she were following her personal compass, she would never risk losing her children over drinking.* Only an alcoholic would make this kind of a decision.

But Briezzia didn't follow the course her personal compass would have set. *She followed the direction set by her addiction.* She continued to drink and the inevitable happened—she lost her children. This created a crisis that eventually propelled her into treatment. In every crisis there is opportunity. Briezzia worked hard while in treatment and completed the program with a commitment to go to any lengths to stay sober. Her willingness to risk losing custody of her children made her recognize the power of her alcoholism. She got honest with herself. In recovery she began the journey of reuniting with her lost true-self, and with her children.

Emotional Sobriety and Our Personal Compass

Let's look at how the concept of a personal compass applies to our emotional sobriety. Once again, emotional sobriety requires that we hold on to ourselves, that we maintain a relationship with ourselves. This means that we honor our true-self and all that entails. We honor both our need to be ourselves and our need for togetherness. We honor our desire to grow and self-actualize. We integrate the seemingly disparate parts of ourselves. We honor all of ourselves. In fact, Dr. Fritz Perls defined mental health as "an appropriate balance of the coordination of all of what we are" (1969, 6). Anything other than honoring ourselves completely is self-hate, self-diminution. It's an act against our true-self.

Therefore, *true north points toward integration.* This is also the goal of therapy. As Dr. Erving Polster said, the goal of psychotherapy is "to merge the disharmonious aspects of the person so that they [can] become joint contributors to the person's wholeness" (2005, 13). We have to integrate our various selves and our basic life forces into a coordinated whole. It's not enough to give one part of us a voice. We won't be spiritually whole until we integrate the counterpoint, or the other part of ourselves, as well. We saw this with Sal: When he moved to integrate his creative woodworking urge with his urge to please his father (his urge to show loyalty), his depression lifted. And we saw this with Briezzia: When she got honest about the role of addiction in thwarting her maternal drive, she began the journey toward sobriety and toward reunification with her children. As I indicated earlier, we naturally and reflexively move in the direction of wholeness, to finish unfinished business, to grow, and to develop.

Emotional dependency undermines this process. It interferes with our growth and development. We lose our autonomy as our false-self pulls our personal compass away from true north. We become control freaks, and we lose trust in ourselves and in the process of life. We forget that the only thing we are really in control of is our effort and our willingness. Nothing more, but nothing less.

So how do we know that we are following true north? We have to check in with ourselves. We have to ask ourselves the question and listen to our answer. We ask, *Is this important to me? Is this in my best interest? Is this what I want? If I let my best self decide, what would I do?*

You see, I believe that we all have an organic wisdom. If we listen to ourselves, our deep wisdom will tell us if the direction we are heading or choice we are making is right for us. Our awareness will tell us the answer to the question. By awareness, I mean that when we ask questions like those above, we will become conscious of feelings that help us know the answers. These feelings will tell us if it we are heading in the right direction.

This is what makes self-awareness important to emotional sobriety. Awareness is the natural magnetic pole that keeps our compass directed toward true north—that keeps us in touch with our true-self. Awareness helps us maintain a relationship with ourselves. If we really listen to ourselves, we are going to know, really know, whether what we are doing is right for us. If the direction we are heading is our true north, it will feel right.

This doesn't imply that we are always going to feel comfortable when we are heading true north. We won't. There will be times when we are uncomfortable and when this discomfort is right for us. When we make a choice to face something that is difficult to face about ourselves, we won't feel comfortable. When we choose to make amends for something we have done wrong, we won't feel comfortable. When we try something new, we won't feel comfortable. When we reach out for help or when we sit down and write out our Fourth Step, we won't feel comfortable. But being willing to be uncomfortable will eventually increase our comfort. Our comfort zone will increase when we face and integrate disowned parts of ourselves.

Jeremy had been seeing me on and off for several years. He was a fireman in his early thirties and had never been married. He had been engaged for about six months and was getting married in June—now just three months away. But something wasn't right. He wasn't excited. He was having more and more doubts about marrying Elizabeth. But he didn't know if this was his fear speaking to him or if there were legitimate reasons he was feeling this way. He wanted my help.

I asked him to have a dialogue between these two parts of himself, the part that wanted to get married and the other side that was doubtful. What he discovered prevented him from making a serious mistake. When he spoke for the part of himself that wanted to get married, he said things like, "It's my obligation," "I gave her my word," "I don't want to let her family down," "It would disappoint so many people if we didn't get married," and "We have sent out the invitations." When he let the side of himself speak, he said one thing and one thing only: "I don't love her."

Many people get married for the wrong reasons. Jeremy might have been one of them if he had not listened to himself. When he vocalized what he had been thinking, that he didn't love her, he knew what he had to do. He knew that he couldn't marry her. This was a very difficult decision, no question about it. But if Jeremy didn't honor himself, he would have made a terrible mistake. He asked Elizabeth to join him in one of our sessions. She was devastated at his news, but when he finally was honest and told her that he didn't love her, believe it or not, it helped. She had enough self-esteem not to want a loveless marriage.

Jeremy listened to himself and found the courage to follow true north. He recognized that he wasn't being truthful to himself nor to Elizabeth. This was a painful realization, and I am certain you can imagine the pressure he felt to sell out. But he didn't. He kept his autonomy. He maintained a relationship with himself and, though difficult, kept his personal integrity.

This story has a happy ending. Jeremy and Elizabeth are now married to other partners, have children, and both seem to be happy. Situations like this don't always end up so well, but this one did. And to a large degree, I attribute the positive outcome to how Jeremy dealt with it.

Here are a few things to check out with yourself to see if you are following or listening to your personal compass:

- Are you living *your* life, or do you feel that you are living the life that other people want you to live?

- When you are helping your partner, are you doing so because *you* choose to or are you helping them because you feel obligated to meet their expectations?
- Are you passionate about your life? Do you look forward to your future with a sense of wonderment?
- Do you work your AA, NA, or Al-Anon program because it is important to you, or are you working your program because it is important to your family?

If you aren't *in* your life, then you aren't listening to your personal compass. You are living the life that you are expected to, and it just won't work. You can only achieve emotional sobriety if you are living your life, rather than meeting someone else's expectations.

Your personal compass can help you stay centered. It can be your personal guide when troubles arise. When you are listening to yourself and following your personal compass, you will feel that it is the right thing to do. You will be in harmony with yourself. It will be right for all of you. When we listen to our true-self, we will intuitively know how to deal with situations that would otherwise baffle us.

Our personal compass is an important piece of equipment to take on our journey. It can help us navigate difficult terrain and get us through troubled waters. It can help us maintain a relationship with ourselves and achieve emotional sobriety.

In the next chapter, I will discuss how to use the tension from the inevitable conflict that occurs in our relationships to facilitate our emotional sobriety.

Smart Thing 11
Embrace Relationship Tensions as the Fuel for Personal Growth

Emotional sobriety develops as we learn how to face life on life's terms. The primary lesson underlying much of what we've learned has been that *we need to nourish a relationship with ourselves.* That is, we each have a hidden true-self, and we must love, understand, and support that long-buried self as it struggles to emerge and thrive.

Paradoxically, one of the great opportunities for nourishing our relationship with ourselves comes through our relationship struggles with other people, especially our intimate partners. These struggles and battles can be a window into the deep needs and unfinished business our true-self seeks to fulfill and resolve.

Trouble in a relationship doesn't necessarily mean that something is wrong with the relationship. Rather, trouble means that something is right. This sounds strange, doesn't it? It did to me when I first encountered this idea. The reason that this sounds so weird to us is that we have been raised in a culture that has many twisted ideas. Our culture is pain phobic. Many of us have been conditioned to see pain as bad, and therefore we avoid suffering the pains of growing up. We demand everything to be as we want it to be, and we insist that it happen right now. We are culturally conditioned to expect the impossible as we search for the easier, softer way. But we pay an incredible price emotionally and spiritually for this cultural myopia.

By accepting these cultural proscriptions uncritically, we have become emotionally immature. And there is no clearer evidence of this immaturity than in how we behave in relationships. We demand, either overtly or covertly, that our partners live up to our expectations. We do the "If you loved me" routine. We have learned to emotionally blackmail the people close to us to get them to behave the way we want them to. We do this because we are emotionally dependent on them for our self-esteem.

Emotional dependency is a symptom of emotional immaturity. Our emotional dependency eventually turns relationships into a source of personal validation rather than a source of enjoyment and knowledge. This acts like a cancer on our relationships, eating away the joy, destroying the friendship, straining our love, destroying sex, and ultimately ruining what we set out to create.

When we are emotionally dependent, we relate to people in terms of what they can or cannot do for our self-esteem. We place the unreasonable demand on our partners to behave in a manner that validates us, and then we get upset when they don't live up to our expectations. And what is even more frustrating is that as someone becomes more important to us, our demands increase, as do the difficulties and conflicts in the relationship.

This usually happens because we re-create the emotional climate of our family of origin with our most intimate partners. Now why on the earth would we try to repeat what originally caused some of our problems? For one thing, as dysfunctional as these patterns of relating may be, they're familiar—we know what to expect. There is another very good answer to this question, though. *We re-create these patterns to give ourselves a chance to work through them*. It is a natural urge for us to complete unfinished business, to move toward closure. This basic need is hardwired into our consciousness.

Augustus Napier, Ph.D., and Carl Whitaker, M.D., two pioneers in family therapy, have said that we pick our partners with an "unconscious wisdom" (1978). *This means that we choose a partner who will create trouble.* Not just any trouble, but the trouble we need to take the next step in our personal development.

Yet we only realize the natural therapeutic benefit of a relationship if we stay in contact with our partner while also maintaining a relationship with ourselves. Now this sounds quite simple, doesn't it? And it *is* a simple concept, but doing it is another matter altogether.

Erin and Keith had been married for twenty years when they came to see me. Erin was in severe crisis. She had had it with Keith and she was not hesitating in letting him know it. In our first session, I had to struggle with her to say anything or give her any feedback. She was on a mission and now she had a captive audience. She wanted to let Keith know what a mess her life was in and the terrible state of their marriage. She went on a tirade about what a loser he was and how horrible their marriage had been for the past eighteen years. She was so upset that she wondered aloud whether she had ever really loved him.

Keith just sat there, dumbfounded. He looked like a truck had just run him over. I guess one did—it was named Erin. He was speechless. But his silence said a lot too. He was confused about what was happening between him and Erin. Their relationship didn't seem that bad to him, a perception that was clearly a part of the problem.

He wasn't emotionally present with Erin. She had done as most partners do in the early stages of a relationship: She reacted to Keith's emotional absence by being accommodating. She tried harder and harder to please him and make up for what was missing. But enough was enough. She wasn't going to function like that anymore.

Predictably, Erin had been in this role her entire life, since childhood. Her father hadn't been emotionally available for her mother, and Erin had compensated by becoming her mother's confidante and emotional support. While it had made her feel important in one way, she resented it as well. She felt like she had lost some of her childhood.

Keith, on the other hand, had grown up in a family that operated from a "power-over," or dominance, mentality. This means that Keith learned to relate from a vertical rather than horizontal position in relationships. It was about who was right or who was wrong. It was about having power over another person, which meant winning arguments at all costs. Now, as a partner and father, Keith demanded blind obedience. He was a tyrant. He bossed around Erin and his children. He was always right, never wrong; he never apologized and had little empathy for how his behavior affected his wife or children.

Erin and Keith had three sons. All three boys had trouble relating to their father. But each of them dealt with their difficulty differently. Tyler withdrew. He had very little interaction with his father. Kevin fought with and rebelled against his father. Meanwhile, James tried hard to please his father. But deep down none of them felt good about their relationship with their dad. Erin hated how alienated they were from their father. This fed her resentment. Although each of the boys was doing the best they could in dealing with Keith, it wasn't nearly enough. Their mother couldn't really help them find a better way to deal with their feelings toward their father because she was struggling with the same issue. She was stuck too.

Now take a moment and consider what kind of profession Keith would feel an affinity toward. If you were thinking that it would be something that was based on a position of authority, you would be right. He was a police officer. He was well prepared for this profession as a child. He operated well in a power-over profession, evidenced by his many accomplishments and promotions. But this mentality didn't serve him well at home.

Let's consider the unconscious wisdom of Keith and Erin—the wisdom in each of them that is seeking their true-selves. Seen from this perspective, Keith chose Erin because he needed someone to challenge his power-over way of being. This was his next developmental step: to find a better way of being in relationship to his wife and children. The power-over approach simply didn't work in intimate, family relationships. But unless he was challenged by someone he loved, he would never have stopped long enough to look at what he was doing. Erin stopped him. She stopped him dead in his tracks. He loved her and didn't want to lose her. Her outrageousness threw him into a personal crisis.

Erin's choice of Keith as a partner also had its own unconscious wisdom, about which we'll learn more in a moment. Let's continue with Keith.

Now trust me when I say it wasn't easy for Keith to come to therapy in the first place. It went against his concept of a "being a man." He had problems with getting marriage counseling on several levels. First, he had to admit that something was wrong with his marriage and with how he functioned as a husband and father. This wasn't at all easy for Keith. However, and to his credit, Keith had enough courage to face that he needed help—partly because in our first session, I helped Keith see that he had a two-choice dilemma. Either path he chose would be accompanied by pain and difficulty. If he didn't face these issues, he would surely lose Erin. This would be devastating. But if he faced the issues she was confronting him about, it would also be difficult and painful. His desire to stay with Erin was stronger than his desire to "be right." He chose to continue marriage counseling.

The second challenge Keith faced was that at the beginning of therapy, Keith wouldn't have been able to recognize a feeling if it hit him on the side of the head. Erin kept asking him how he felt, and he didn't know how to answer her. At times it seemed like his wife and children were speaking a different language. Well, in fact, they were. Emotions were a personal language that Keith had never learned.

A turning point in his therapy came when Keith started talking about what it was like for him as a child. Predictably, he had learned this power-over way of functioning from his dad. His dad was a tyrant. His mother submitted to her husband's tyranny. Keith often felt oppressed and put down by his father. He could never do anything right. His father rarely recognized Keith's achievements and didn't know how to appreciate his individuality. I pointed out to him that he was doing something very similar to his family. Keith started to cry when he realized that this is what he had been doing to his wife and children.

Erin's own unconscious growth needs demanded a partner who would re-create the same issue that she had in her family, so that she could find a better way to deal with it. She needed to learn how to confront this emotional dynamic without submitting and losing herself. She needed to learn how to stay connected and keep her integrity. She had never learned this growing up.

I often tell my patients that the most common diagnosis I see is ignorance. Yes, people suffer from depression or anxiety and other psychiatric issues, but the underlying problem is usually that we have never learned how to live a better life. We could only learn what our parents knew to teach us, which is never enough. Rather than focusing on the pathology, I prefer to start from the premise that our partners are heaven-sent to help us learn these unlearned lessons. That was the journey that Keith and Erin were on.

Though Keith was initially reluctant to take this journey, he hung in there, and the results have been incredible for him. He surrendered to the tension of his marital crisis and used it to help him take the next step in his development. Today, he is learning a new way of being and communicating with his wife and his children.

Erin's bitterness and contempt for Keith has now dissipated. It was replaced with a compassion for Keith. But she found her voice too. She learned from their conflict how to ask for what she wants and to stand up for herself and her needs, rather than just accommodate Keith's needs all the time. This had a remarkable effect on Erin. She is reinvigorated, reenergized. She looks forward to her future with Keith rather than dreading it.

Again, relationships are people growers. But only through struggles with our partner will we reap the natural therapeutic benefits of our relationships. As I stated in my book *Love Secrets Revealed*, "We pick someone who, by his or her very nature, will furnish us with an opportunity to master the as-yet unaltered, to encourage us to give a voice to the as-yet unspeakable, to insist that we take another step forward in the endless pursuit of personal development and personal integrity" (2006, 5).

By keeping ourselves pressed up against the struggle we are having with our partner, we will grow. We will learn how to maintain contact with our partner while simultaneously maintaining autonomy. We will learn how to keep our individuality while maintaining contact. Now, this can't be taught. It can only be learned. The energy from the fire of discord in our relationship helps us develop this ability. If we hang in there with the right attitude, we will learn to repair ourselves and hold on to ourselves.

This is not the idealized romantic image perpetuated by our culture. We don't fall in love and live happily ever after. That idealized image has confused love with dependency. Dependency is not love;

it is emotional fusion. Love encourages freedom, choice, passion, experimentation, and exploration. It doesn't want to control anyone or anything. It is generous and fearless. But dependency engenders the opposite energy. Dependency demands control, predictability, rigidity, and submission. It is fear-based.

A healthy relationship is not based on dependency or on self-sacrifice. Quite the contrary. A healthy relationship requires that we put more of ourselves into our relationship, not less. Our culture's romantic ideals say we should sacrifice ourselves for the sake of love, that love is selfless, but when selflessness is equated with sacrificing our true selves, this is wrong. Standing on our own two feet forms the basis of adult love. Recall what I've noted previously: Erich Fromm, M.D., referred to adult love as "mature love." He defined mature love as "union with the preservation of integrity" (1956).

Mature love is based on choice rather than dependency. Mature love says, "I want you because I love you," rather than, "I love you because I need you." Our level of differentiation determines the type of love experience we will have in our relationships. The more differentiated we are, the more we can keep our individuality and encourage our partner to do likewise. The less differentiated we are, the more we will lose our individuality to "togetherness" and require— no, *demand*—our partner to do likewise.

Conflict in a relationship can help us forge a better relationship with ourselves and with our partners. Handled maturely and responsibly, conflict can help us grow up emotionally and learn how to hold on to ourselves while we keep ourselves pressed up against the tension. If you are struggling with an ongoing problem in a relationship and you aren't making any progress, get some help; the struggle is your opening to uncover and release your true-self. A good therapist can help you with this.

We have discussed eleven smart things that you can do to

strengthen your emotional sobriety and hence your recovery. In the next chapter, we will discuss another must for your emotional sobriety tool box. It's based on the idea that the problem is never what we believe it to be. The real problem comes from the way we respond to problems.

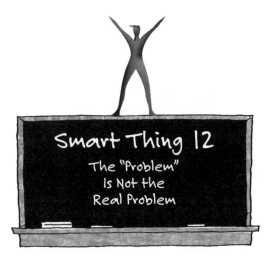

Smart Thing 12

The "Problem" Is Not the Real Problem

As you have seen throughout this book, emotional sobriety is the result of a new way of being. It's a new way of looking at life and a new way of looking at ourselves. If we commit ourselves to this journey, we will use our personal compass to guide ourselves in new directions. We will move toward being more thoughtful, and move away from being reactive. We will move toward integrity, and move away from playing games with ourselves and others. We will move toward our true-self, and move away from our idealized or false-self. We will move away from perfectionism, and move toward appreciating progress. We will strive to maintain a relationship with ourselves, to honor ourselves, and move away from betraying and abandoning ourselves.

Our growth along these lines is ongoing. Emotional sobriety is not an event; it is a *process*. We will never master emotional sobriety, but we will learn to grow it from our mistakes and experiences. Our efforts will help us develop a new level of compassion for ourselves and for others.

Sounds great, doesn't it? It is, and it can happen to you if you work for it! If you are willing to experiment with some of the suggestions in this book, you will begin to discover how to hold on to yourself. You will learn how to take charge of your emotions rather than letting your emotions drive you. The quality of your life will improve.

But there is one more smart thing I want to discuss in this book. I want to help you understand what creates the problems in our life. I want you to look at the very notion of "problems" from a different perspective and to see that the *problem*—whatever problem you think you have—is most often *not* the real problem. What you've identified as the problem is really a sign that something is lacking in your life. The "something missing" is the real problem and is a key to regaining your true-self. Your job, in seeking emotional sobriety, is to find out what's missing.

Let's start by looking at some of the things that people identify as a problem when they come to therapy. I ask people to tell me what they believe is the biggest problem in their life, today. Here are some of the answers I typically receive:

- I am depressed.
- I am anxious.
- I drink too much or I use drugs too much.
- My partner had an affair.
- My partner is verbally abusive.
- My partner has no interest in sex.
- I am thinking about getting a divorce.
- I don't like my job.
- I relapsed.
- I am numb.
- I don't like how much I worry about things.
- I am indecisive.

- I am lonely.
- I want to lose weight.
- I have a terrible relationship with my children.
- My partner is just beginning recovery.
- I am having trouble with one of my children.
- I don't like my mother or father.
- My partner doesn't listen to me.

As a therapist, I was trained to listen to what a person is *not* saying. To listen to what is not being said is a cool idea, isn't it? I thought so the first time I heard it. What a person *doesn't* say is as important as what they say, if not more so. I have learned that listening to what my clients don't say is key to identifying the next step in their development: What is missing helps me see the "holes" in their personal development or maturation.

Now, of course, we don't actually have holes in our personality. What we have are holes in our ability to function. Let's say I didn't want to see certain things growing up, because I was too vulnerable. As an adult, then, I might not be able to see reality because I simply didn't learn how—I would have a deficit or a block in what I am willing to look at. I heard one of my patients say, "I don't *see* what I look at." For example, if I heard certain things going on in my family when I was growing up that caused me anxiety, I may have a hole in my ability to hear certain things that cause me anxiety as an adult. If I didn't want to feel at all, then I would have a hole in my heart. Think of these holes as functional deficits. These deficits limit our ability to cope. If I have trained myself to "not see" certain things, then my ability to cope with any situation that includes those things will be compromised.

We can also think of this as amputating parts of ourselves—we cut off the parts that we don't like or that we are told are no good.

We cut off our feelings; we cut off seeing reality; we cut off our anger. The list of things we cut off is endless. These amputations limit our functioning, just as though we had an arm or a leg amputated. While we'd eventually adjust to the loss of an arm, we'd never function as well without it.

How is that we end up with these holes in our development? It happens because we have alienated or disowned various parts of ourselves in order to live up to our idealized self-image—in order to make ourselves more acceptable and lovable. Let's say I am "supposed" to be understanding and compassionate. In order to be this way, I have to disown any part of me that doesn't meet these specifications. Therefore, I can't be impatient or annoyed with you, even if you are really annoying me. There's no room for this reaction in my personality. So I project these feelings and deny them.

The process of projecting or disowning these parts of myself creates holes in my functioning. If something or someone annoys me, I won't allow myself to feel annoyed. If I don't recognize that I am feeling annoyed, then I am unable to take care of myself. I am unable to assert myself and do something about what is happening. I will have to work around my true feelings, and this avoidance turns me into a phony. Maybe I will numb myself and not make myself sensitive to being annoyed, or I might see everyone else as being impatient or annoyed, or I might become a "nice guy" who is never annoyed or frustrated.

I hope a machine will someday be invented that can do an X-ray or MRI of the psyche to measure these psychological holes in our personality. I think such a machine would produce scans that resembled Swiss cheese for most of us.

The more holes we have in our cheese, the less differentiated we are. The more holes, the more rigidity we will have in our personalities. The holes in our personality cause stereotyped behavior. They decrease freedom and restrict our responses because certain behaviors or actions are defined as off limits. I remember the T-shirt a patient was wearing who attended one of my lectures at the National Council of Alcoholism and Drug Addiction. It said, "Before you even ask, the answer is NO!" This is stereotyped behavior. He always said NO; he didn't have a YES in his life. There was a hole where the YES should have been. The more holes we have in our personality, the less ability we have to deal with life on life's terms. Fritz Perls once said, "We have to lose our mind so that we can come to our senses" (1973).

Louie came to see me because his wife, Carmen, who was a dentist, was in a ninety-day treatment program for health care professionals. Louie said he didn't know how to resolve his anger and resentment toward Carmen. He wanted to let go of these feelings but couldn't. Here's what Louie told me.

Louie loved Carmen very much. He fell head over heels for her. She was a very successful orthodontist who attended Al-Anon meetings—her ex-husband had died from alcoholism. Louie was in recovery. He was sober for fifteen years when they started dating. Louie was a traveling salesman who sold surgical equipment. Carmen was very busy with her successful orthodontic practice and with raising two young daughters.

After being happily married for five years, Carmen started coming home later and later. When Louie questioned her, she would explain that either she was tied up at work with an emergency or she had to complete some patient charts. Louie didn't give it a second thought at first. He trusted Carmen. But he became more and more suspicious the longer this went on and silently doubted what she was telling him. He wondered how she could have this many emergencies or why she couldn't bring her charts home. But he didn't talk to her about it. He just silently wondered what this really meant. You wouldn't have been able to tell that Louie was having his doubts, because he acted like he believed Carmen.

Louie knew something wasn't right, but he didn't have any concrete evidence to support his suspicions. At times he imagined that Carmen was having an affair. But he felt a pressure to trust her. It was the right thing and the loving thing to do, and anyway he knew Carmen loved him. Every now and again he would hint at his suspicion with her, and she would reassure him. "I am not having an affair," she insisted. "I love you."

This was the truth; Carmen wasn't having an affair. But what Carmen didn't tell her husband was that she had become dependent on a short-acting opiate that she used for anesthesia at the office. She rarely drank alcohol, but one day she used this drug to treat a bad headache. She loved the feeling. She felt so serene and peaceful—a feeling that her type A personality seldom allowed her to experience. She was immediately hooked and soon lost control.

This is the last problem Louie would have suspected. Carmen wasn't working late; she was passing out at the office after getting high. That's why she was coming home at unusual hours.

Louie didn't *see* what was really going on with Carmen. His blind spot was created by two things. First, Carmen fooled him. She was very convincing and she could have passed a lie detector test. Unfortunately, the art of deception is one thing that we addicts become very good at. Second, Louie didn't want to see that there was a problem. He had selective inattention. He didn't want to believe that Carmen was less than perfect. He was emotionally dependent on her. He needed her to be the healthy one, the strong one, the capable and stable one. He had borrowed his own feelings of strength and stability from her strength and stability.

Since being with Carmen, his career and life were soaring. He attributed much of his success and happiness to Carmen and her influence on him. Louie didn't discover the truth until one night in late September. He had been calling Carmen since 9 p.m., and it was now after midnight. He was worried sick that something horrible had happened to her. He didn't know what to do. He imagined that something terrible had happened. First he thought that she had been in an auto accident, so he started calling the local hospitals to see if she had been admitted. But there was no record of her admission. Next he envisioned someone breaking into her office to steal narcotics and hurting her during the robbery. In his mind's eye, he saw her lying in a pool of blood, needing help. He wanted to rush out of the house and go to her office, but he didn't dare leave her daughters at home alone. Instead, he called the police. It was midnight. The police officers gained access to Carmen's office and found her passed out with a needle in her arm. They called the paramedics, and Carmen was taken to a local ER to be treated for an overdose.

Louie was furious that Carmen had been lying to him. He took it personally. Carmen went to treatment the next day, and Louie was referred to me for help.

As I mentioned earlier, when Louie and I started working together, the first issue he wanted to discuss was his feelings of resentment and anger for being betrayed. Louie didn't trust Carmen anymore. How could he? She had repeatedly lied to him. These feeling had grown into resentment and turned into a seething contempt toward her. They were tearing Louie apart and affecting Carmen as well. But remember, I said that the "problem" is not the real problem. Louie thought his problem was the feelings of anger and resentment, and his sense that he could not let go of those feelings. The real problem was deeper.

I hope that as you were reading Louie's story, you were also asking yourself what was missing from Louie's behavior. I had a lot of empathy for Louie. I could easily put myself in his shoes and understand the betrayal he felt. He thought Carmen was trust-worthy. He had no reason to believe otherwise. But as you are about to find out, there were holes in Louie's personality that prevented him from holding on to himself. That was Louie's real problem—not the perfectly natural anger and resentment.

You see, among other things, Louie believed that Carmen would never fall prey to addiction. He mistakenly concluded that Carmen's painful experiences with her deceased husband would protect her from this disease. He repeatedly expressed his dismay over Carmen's drug use despite her experience with her first husband's drinking. Yet if anyone could understand how the disease of addiction corrupts one's integrity and overrides our best thinking, it should have been Louie—he'd been there.

Louie was a recovering alcoholic who had lied to his ex-wife thousands of times about his drinking, just as Carmen had lied to him about her drug use. Plus, Louie's father was an alcoholic, but that didn't prevent him from becoming an alcoholic. I pointed these things out to Louie. Sometimes the obvious is not so obvious. This awareness helped Louie begin to connect the dots. As a result, he started to have more compassion for Carmen. But what finally resolved Louie's resentment toward Carmen was when he confronted himself and began to look at the ways that he had betrayed himself. He looked at the holes in his functioning.

Remember, whatever we think our partner is doing to us, we are probably doing the same thing to ourselves. Such was the case with Louie. In one of our sessions, when he was talking about how Carmen had ruined his trust, I said, "You keep talking about how Carmen has betrayed you, but I wonder if you aren't upset with yourself too?"

He paused, looked at me knowingly, and then said, "I know that where there is smoke there is fire. I'm not stupid. But I kept telling myself that there wasn't a problem, that I was making it all up. I didn't trust myself. I usually don't trust myself. I didn't want to believe that something was threatening our life together. I didn't want to believe that something was wrong, so I put my head in the sand."

What an incredible admission. This was fantastic. We were making progress.

Louie recounted several signs of trouble that he saw but never mentioned to Carmen. He saw the tracks in her arms, needles in her briefcase, and drugs in her purse. Louie colluded with Carmen because he didn't want to face what was happening. His denial matched Carmen's denial. They were both in denial, and they were both betrayed by themselves and each other.

When Louie stepped up and recognized that he had betrayed himself, his resentment toward Carmen dissipated. He no longer focused on Carmen's trustworthiness, but instead focused on his inability to trust himself. *This inability to trust himself was the real problem.* It revealed the holes in his personality. He gave up being a victim—a move that was long overdue—and focused on the important job of filling in the holes in his personality. He started filling in his self-worth hole and addressing his emotional dependency on Carmen. He started filling in the "don't talk about what you are feeling" hole and found his voice. He started filling in the lack-of-self-trust hole and started validating himself. He put the pressure on himself to change instead of pressuring Carmen to change.

Carmen worked hard in treatment and benefited tremendously. When she was discharged, she joined Louie in therapy with me, and they began the task of reconstructing their relationship.

Louie's work on himself and Carmen's recovery had a major impact on their lives. It shifted the dynamics of their marriage in a very positive direction. They were much more authentic with each other. Their love matured. At first Carmen seemed threatened that

Louie was no longer emotionally dependent on her. But eventually she began to enjoy the new connection. Louie also enjoyed his new-found self-worth.

As we have seen, the holes in Louie's personality made it difficult for him to cope with Carmen and her addiction. They blinded him to her addiction, despite the evidence. The holes in our personality interfere with our ability to be fully present—to be right here, right now.

The more we are living in the moment and the more of our true-selves we have to bring to the moment, the more responsive we will be to whatever a situation demands for us to do to hold on to ourselves.

If Louie had been more present to what was happening in his marriage, he would have induced a crisis in their relationship much earlier. He would have been more responsive to what was going on rather than talk himself out of what he saw. This is what I meant when I said that we need to add more of ourselves to our lives to create emotional sobriety.

When we function from our true-self, we will cope with problems with the best and most relevant parts of ourselves. We won't let the holes in our personality dictate how we respond to a problem. As the brilliant therapist Virginia Satir stated, "The problem is not the problem. The problem is coping" (1972). Coping is hampered when we have holes in our personality. When we disown who we are, we can never cope that well with life. Life requires all hands on deck.

Throughout this book, we have explored many different ways to cope with the feelings or problems we encounter at work, in relationships, or in maintaining a relationship with ourselves. Here are a few tips for handling an impasse with a problem. Remember, what you think is the problem is not necessarily the real problem. The actions below are designed to help you discover the real problem. They help you stop, step back from the thing that's bothering you, and look for the emotional dependency underlying your reaction.

- *Do something different.* Doing the same thing and expecting different results is the definition of insanity. A good rule of thumb is to do something that is 180 degrees out from what you have been doing. If you are hard, soften yourself. If you are passive, become proactive. If you are reactive, become thoughtful. If you are a pushover, become assertive. If you are paralyzed with fear, be daring and outrageous. If you are too serious, lighten up. Consider the opposite of what you typically do.
- *Reconsider issues, options, and solutions that you rejected as unacceptable or undoable in the past.* In order to do this, ask yourself what you would have to change about yourself or what you would have to accept or give up for this to become a real option. Maybe you will discover that what you need to give up is something that is worth letting go of and that you would like yourself more if you could do this.
- *Stop "awfulizing."* Accept the present reality as it is and settle down. Quiet yourself with a prayer or meditation instead of exacerbating your anxious state of mind.
- *Focus on containing your behavior when you are having trouble soothing yourself.* Don't make things harder on yourself than they need to be. Remind yourself that this too shall pass. Take things one moment at a time.
- *Let the best of you do the thinking and talking.* Stay committed to letting the best of you stay in the lead during a crisis or when struggling with an ongoing problem. Use your personal compass to keep moving toward true north.

- *Focus on the solution.* Stop playing the blame game. Blame will only make it more difficult to find a solution. Choose to be a part of the solution instead of contributing to the problem.
- *Don't sweat the small stuff.* Ask yourself if this issue is of critical importance. Is the issue one of ultimate concern? If it is, hold your ground; it's worth the struggle. If it's not, then it is likely your need to be right and your false pride is keeping you stuck.
- *Get some distance from the issue.* Sleep on the problem. Very few things need to be resolved immediately. Take a time-out. Oftentimes creating some distance from a problem can help you gain a better perspective or calm down.
- *Listen to yourself.* Don't get lost in the situation. You may already have the answer to a problem. You just have to listen to yourself to uncover it.
- *Be personal when discussing the problem.* Communicate what you want, what you'd like, or what you don't want or don't like. Don't criticize and avoid asking questions; instead make statements. Be direct and clear.
- *Pay attention to the tone of your voice.* Nonverbal communication is very powerful. How you communicate is as important as what you say.
- *Challenge your expectations and identify your emotional dependency.* It's fine to have rules and principles to guide your behavior. But expecting other people to do it your way is unreasonable and creates lots of trouble.
- *Don't forget to laugh and enjoy the journey.* No one is perfect. We all make mistakes. When you catch yourself trying to be perfect, laugh it off. Don't take yourself too seriously.

- *Ask for help.* Just because you have tried everything you know, it doesn't mean that the situation is hopeless. New information can help unlock gridlock.

Correctly assessing when to act versus when to accept a situation is an important aspect of emotional sobriety. The actions above help you gain perspective on the problem as it first presents itself, so that you can find the real "hole" beneath the problem. This work also helps you achieve emotional sobriety, because it helps you see how your emotional dependency controls you.

There is one final action, well-known to recovering people: I encourage you to use the Serenity Prayer often when you are lost or confused or struggling with an impasse. It's a wonderful and useful tool.

God, grant me the serenity to accept the things I cannot change, the courage to change the things I can, and the wisdom to know the difference.

Serenity, courage, and wisdom are your allies in learning to live with yourself and your emotional dependency—even as you seek greater emotional sobriety. Now that we've covered the twelve smart things that can lay a foundation for emotional sobriety, I'd like to close by creating a vision for you; then we'll finish filling out the fifth column of the Emotional Sobriety Inventory Form.

A Vision for You
Putting All the Pieces Together

Breaking the bond of addiction is merely the beginning of our journey in recovery. This has been referred to as Stage I recovery by Earnie Larsen (1985). Have no doubt about the importance of this stage of recovery. It is the foundation for our program of recovery.

Surrendering to the reality that we are powerless over alcohol and other drugs marks the beginning of recovery and is unquestionably necessary before we can get on with the task of growing up. Think of surrender as the mortar of recovery. It cements the building blocks of our foundation: humility, honesty, open-mindedness, and willingness to change. The strength and character of our foundation determines the degree of stability of our recovery. The stronger our foundation, the more stable our recovery.

It is crucial to accept our powerlessness over alcohol and other drugs. I have witnessed hundreds of men and women who have tried to prove otherwise, to prove that they were normal and therefore could drink or use and control it. They weren't willing to accept that they were bodily and mentally different from their friends or family. They wanted to believe that they could enjoy drinking or using like they had at some point in their past. Unfortunately, none was successful; all paid a terrible price. Their refusal to surrender caused their foundations to crumble. Some even paid the price with their lives.

Once we surrender, we stop struggling with the reality of our compulsion and obsession to drink or use. The mortar of our foundation sets, and we can get on with the next step in recovery. Bill Wilson called this step *emotional sobriety*, which he defined as a "real maturity" and "balance" in our relationship with ourselves, our fellows, and our Higher Power. We cannot have balance if we make what other people think or feel more important than what we think or feel. We cannot have balance or hold on to ourselves emotionally if we don't grow up. Therefore, it is best to think about emotional sobriety as a by-product of a particular way of being in our life. Emotional sobriety concerns itself with the emotional quality of our life.

I have written this book to help you acquire some new ways to cope with your emotions in order to help you achieve emotional sobriety. I suggested twelve things that you can do to increase your emotional resilience. They were

1. Know yourself—and how to stay centered.
2. Stop allowing others to edit your reality.
3. Stop taking things personally.
4. Own your projections as an act of integrity.
5. Confront yourself for the sake of your integrity.
6. Stop pressuring others to change, and instead pressure yourself to change.
7. Develop a healthy perspective toward yourself, your feelings, and your emotional themes.
8. Appreciate what is.
9. Comfort yourself when you are hurt or disappointed.
10. Use your personal compass to guide your life.

11. Embrace relationship tensions as the fuel for personal growth.
12. The "problem" is not the real problem.

We are going to refer to these in a minute, but before we do I'd like you to pull out the writing you did in Smart Thing 1 when you filled out the first four columns of the Emotional Sobriety Inventory Form. This form was based on Bill Wilson's observation that "If we examine every disturbance we have, great or small, we will find at the root of it some unhealthy dependency and its consequent unhealthy demand."

If you haven't done the exercise, do it now. Even if you have done it, do it again. It may be interesting to see if you have changed since you first filled out the form. Doing (or repeating) the exercise will help you integrate what you have been learning on both an intellectual and an emotional level.

Just a reminder, the chart looks like this:

The Emotional Sobriety Inventory Form

Upsetting event	Unhealthy dependency	Unreasonable expectation, claim, or demand	Your reaction, or how you responded to the situation	In order to stay centered, I need to realize that _____.

Here is what I'd like you to do. Make several copies of the Emotional Sobriety Inventory Form on page 173. Over the next twenty-four hours, record anything and everything that either upsets you or bothers you. Do not omit any reaction. Record these events or describe these situations in the first column. Let's say that you just put down this book and were ready to climb into bed. A good friend calls. She tells you that she has to cancel breakfast with you tomorrow morning, but she doesn't give you a reason. She then hurries off the phone and tells you that she will call you later in the week to reschedule. Usually this doesn't bother you, but tonight you got upset. Write this down in the first column.

In columns 2 and 3, you are going to ask yourself two different but related questions. First, "What is the unhealthy dependency that is underlying my emotional reaction?" Second, "What is the unreasonable expectation or demand that my unhealthy dependency is generating?"

If you felt upset that your friend canceled because you had something important you wanted to talk over with her, then the unhealthy dependency might be "I rely on my friend to help me deal with my confusion about setting boundaries in my relationship with people I really care about." The unreasonable expectation that may be spawned by your emotional dependency may be something like, "I demand that she is always be available, whenever I need her, regardless of what is going on in her life."

Next, in column 4, write down how you reacted to the person or situation. Let's say you got angry with your friend and then said something to yourself like, "I'm not going to answer her call when she contacts me to reschedule." (As we learned, this withdrawal is called *moving away*.) Or you might have said something like, "I am going to call her back tomorrow and give her a piece of my mind." (This kind of attack, as you recall, is *moving against*.) Or you might have thought something like, "I am not very good company; I have too many problems. That's why my friend canceled our breakfast."

(Remember, this kind of submission is called *moving toward*.) Whatever your reaction was, write it down. Reread Smart Thing 1 if you'd like more detailed instructions on this exercise.

Now we turn our attention to last column in the Emotional Sobriety Inventory, column 5. This column is about a solution and is concerned with what you need to do to stay centered, to keep your emotional center of gravity within yourself. There are no absolute answers for column 5. What works for you may not work for someone else. You need to discover your personal antidote to emotional dependency. This is where I want you to try on some of the suggestions in this book on the twelve smart things you can do to cope with your emotions.

To ensure that you have found the right solution, experiment with your answer to this question in the fifth column before you conclude that it is a solution. Try it on to see if it actually helps. Listen to yourself as you experiment. If something helps, you will immediately feel different: You will regain your emotional balance, your resentment will dissipate, you will feel centered, you will recover your individuality and keep your autonomy. You will be able to maintain a relationship with yourself and stay pressed up against the situation. So the value of the coping strategy you select will be determined by your emotional response. Your response is the ultimate test of the value of your solution.

Here's an example. Let's say that in reaction to your friend canceling breakfast, you became aware that you were angry with her and wanted to call her up and scold her for not being a very good friend. You might pause and consider that she did what she did because of who she is, not because of who you are. By reflecting on the situation, you might also realize that you didn't let her know that you wanted to talk to her about a situation you were struggling with. She can't be expected to respect your feelings until you respect your own feelings and ask her for what you want. After realizing that you didn't speak up for yourself, you might decide to call your friend and let her know that you'd like to talk with her as soon as possible. Your reaction to this move to take care of yourself will tell you if you found the right antidote. If you have found the right solution for you, you will feel better about yourself. You won't be holding a grudge toward your friend. You will be able to maintain your connection to her and feel good about yourself.

Now take every situation that you listed in the first column and begin to experiment with different antidotes. Imagine yourself to be a scientist looking for the cure to your emotional dependency. Even if something you try doesn't work, it doesn't mean you have failed or that you wasted your time. A failed experiment is still informative. It can tell you what doesn't work for you. This can help you rule out certain coping strategies. Review the chapters covering the twelve smart things, if necessary.

Once you get the hang of this process, you may see a theme emerge around your discoveries for dealing with your emotional dependency. If a theme does emerge, take note of it. In the future you can use this coping strategy first.

A Vision for You

As you have learned, the "problem" is not necessarily the problem. The problem is a hole in ourselves that blinds us to our real feelings and prevents us from expressing our true-selves. Accepting this reality can help us get on with growing up. This is the insight Bill Wilson shared with us in his remarkable letter (see pages 8–12). Instead of blaming others, he decided to take a hard look at how his actions were causing him problems. He couldn't accomplish this alone. He asked for help. He didn't judge himself; he faced his immaturity head-on and learned from it. His personal courage, integrity, and honesty inspired me to follow his lead. I hope Bill inspires you too.

Self-regulation leads to emotional resilience. The more we are able to master our feelings, the more confidence we will have in dealing with life on life's terms. The more resilient we will be when we are knocked off balance. And the quicker we will regain our balance.

Self-mastery shouldn't be confused with self-control. *Self-mastery is not about controlling ourselves. It is about maintaining a healthy relationship with ourselves.* Self-mastery is about coping with our feelings, regulating our reactions, and repairing ourselves. It's about following our true north and letting the best parts of ourselves respond. It's about listening to ourselves and respecting our integrity. It's about accepting and attending to our true-selves rather than trying to control others or circumstances. It's about maintaining our autonomy when we are feeling pressured to give ourselves up. Emotional sobriety is the by-product of learning more effective ways of coping with our feelings.

In order to hold on to ourselves, we need to keep ourselves emotionally centered. We need to surrender our hobbling emotional demands and replace them with healthier, more realistic ideas. This is the path to our emotional sobriety.

As we have discussed, holding on to ourselves involves maintaining a relationship with ourselves. It is not surprising that self-esteem also requires maintaining this relationship. To *esteem* something is to respect it. Self-esteem is another way of saying that we *respect our true-selves.*

Dr. Nathaniel Branden, the self-esteem pioneer I mentioned in the introduction, found that people with high self-esteem do the following six things:

1. They live a conscious life. They do not avoid themselves or run away from difficulties. They have a curiosity about

themselves, their feelings, and their behavior. They seek truth and wisdom, and they are committed to being their best selves.

2. They take total responsibility for their lives, for their happiness, for their self-esteem, for their behavior, and for their feelings.

3. They accept themselves as they are. This doesn't mean that they don't strive for improvement in their lives, because they do, but they don't reject themselves to begin the journey. They start with where they are at and support themselves during the journey.

4. They are appropriately self-assertive, which means that they operate from a principle of mutual respect. They believe, "I am as important you are, not more or less important."

5. They live life with a purpose. They have a reason for their existence. Their life has direction. They aren't floating through life in a rudderless boat. They have discovered their passion and integrate it into their lives.

6. They live life with integrity. This isn't just about morality, although it includes being ethical. It is much more than ethics. They live with an attitude of inclusivity. They honor and respect all of the various parts of themselves. They operate from a state of wholeness.

It seems that people with high self-esteem hold on to themselves, doesn't it?

Dr. Branden said, "This is one of the reasons why attempts at relationships so often fail—not because the vision of passionate or romantic love is intrinsically irrational, but because the self-esteem needed to support it is absent" (1994). Holding on to ourselves is the support we need to support our attempts at relationships.

Recently a friend of mine was diagnosed with cataracts. Cataracts are like having a dull film placed over your eyes. They come on slowly. As the cataracts grew over time, he adjusted to the way they affected his vision. He didn't realize that his vision had changed. Then he had cataract surgery. The ophthalmologist performed the procedure on my friend's left eye first. After the bandage was removed, he could hardly believe what he was seeing. Everything looked crisp, clear, and colorful. When he covered his left eye and looked only through his right eye, everything looked cloudy and colorless. He had been seeing a cloudy, colorless world for years, but it had crept up on him gradually. This was how the world looked because this was how he saw it. He didn't know better until the surgeon cut away the cataracts. With one eye repaired and the other still clouded, he was able to compare the two realities, cloudy and clear, side by side.

Our emotional dependency has the same effect on our perception that cataracts have on our vision. It clouds our emotional perception, and hence it clouds our world.

At an AA meeting, I heard someone say that we have a "disease of perception." I think I understand what she meant. The way we look at life creates problems. But we never consider that our perceptions are so strongly influenced by our emotional dependency. This powerful invisible emotional force determines what we focus on, how we process information, how we make decisions, and even how we react. We uncritically accept this reality just as my friend accepted the clouded world created by his cataracts. We don't know any better, and neither did he.

It would be nice, wouldn't it, if we could simply surgically receive the kind of emotional clarity we seek. In this book, my goal has been to conduct surgery on your vision of yourself, to help you remove the cataracts that have clouded your emotional sobriety.

I learned about this "emotional" surgery because I had to go through it myself. I realized how emotionally dependent I was. It was like I had everything backward. What *was*, wasn't. And what *wasn't*, was. I used to believe that the aim of life was being perfect, that it was about having and possessing. I wanted everything for myself. I believed that perfection and possessing, not sharing, would give me pleasure and satisfaction. I used to believe *the more I have, the more perfect I am.*

I've removed my cataracts. My vision is no longer clouded. Today I see my dependence on possession and perfection as utter nonsense. Recovery has helped me regain the life force that my addiction and false-self hijacked. I am now committed to living a conscious life of loving service. I am a work in progress and will never achieve perfection. Today I strive to be more human. I have learned that the more I give away, the more I have. I have also learned that the more I include my true-self in my life, the more I enjoy life and learn from it.

Dr. Tian Dayton summarized the qualities of emotional sobriety quite well. She stated,

> Emotional sobriety encompasses our ability to live with
> balance and maturity. It means that we have learned to
> keep our emotions, thoughts and actions in a balanced
> range. Our thinking, feeling, and behavior are reasonably
> congruent, and we're not ruled by or held captive by any
> part of us. We don't live in our heads, our emotions don't
> run us, and we aren't overly driven by unconscious or
> compulsive behaviors. We operate from a reasonably inte-
> grated flow and enjoy a life experience that is more or less
> balanced and present oriented. (2007, 1).

Emotional sobriety means holding on to ourselves. This does not mean that we aren't influenced by others, because we will be at times. The issue is how we arrive at being influenced. Letting ourselves be influenced out of choice is very different from being emotionally reactive. The kind of reaction that comes from an intense emotional experience based on being emotionally fused is significantly different from making a choice to be influenced. When we *choose* to be influenced, we retain our individuality. When we choose to go along with a person or situation, we maintain our integrity. Another way of saying this is that we maintain our connection to our individuality.

Emotional sobriety expands our consciousness. It extends our recovery and gives us an emotional resilience. It helps us cope, however life challenges us. Remember the quote I gave you from Dr. Viktor Frankl, a brilliant psychiatrist who survived internment in a German concentration camp during World War II? Frankl noted, "The way in which man accepts his fate and all the suffering it entails, the way he takes up his cross, gives him ample opportunity—even under the most difficult circumstances—to add deeper meaning to his life" (1959, 76).

Dr. Frankl's observations are particularly relevant. He had lived through a horrific crucible that forced him to see life maturely, to appreciate *what is.* When we accept and deal with our emotional dependency, our life and relationships can have a deeper meaning and a greater significance than we ever dreamed possible.

Bill Wilson, in an *AA Grapevine* article entitled "The Greatest Gift of All," left us with a wonderful vision of the possibilities of recovery. He stated,

Sobriety is only the bare beginning. It is only the first gift of the first awakening. If more gifts are to be received, the awakening has to go on. And if it does go on, we find that bit by bit we can discard the old life—the one that didn't work—for a life that does and can work under any conditions whatever. (1957, 234)

That is my vision for you. That sobriety is only your bare beginning. That your sight, clouded so long by emotional dependency, becomes clear. That you find your true-self, accept it, and hold on to it through whatever the world throws at you.

References

Alcoholics Anonymous. 2001. *Alcoholics Anonymous.* New York: Alcoholics Anonymous World Services.

———. 1981. *Twelve steps and twelve traditions.* New York: Alcoholics Anonymous World Services.

Berger, A. 2006. *Love secrets revealed: What happy couples know about having great sex, deep intimacy and a lasting connection.* Deerfield Beach, FL: HCI Books.

———. 2008. *12 stupid things that mess up recovery.* Center City, MN: Hazelden.

Branden, N. 1994. *The six pillars of self-esteem.* New York: Bantam Books.

———. 2010. Personal communication with author (March 29).

Bugental, J. F. T. 1978. *Psychotherapy and process: The fundamentals of an Existential-Humanistic approach.* New York: Random House.

Dayton, T. 2007. *Emotional sobriety: From relationship trauma to resilience and balance.* Deerfield Beach, FL: HCI Books.

Frankl, V. E. 1959. *Man's search for meaning: An introduction to logotherapy.* New York: Simon and Schuster.

Fromm, E. 1956. *The art of loving.* New York: Harper and Row.

Goble, F. 1970, 1971. *The third force: The psychology of Abraham Maslow—A revolutionary new view of man.* New York: Pocket Books.

Gottman, J., and N. Silver. 1999. *The seven principles for making marriage work*. New York: Three Rivers Press.

Horney, K. 1950. *Neurosis and human growth: The struggle toward self-realization*. New York: W.W. Norton.

Kempler, W. 1982. Personal communication with author.

Kerr, M. E., and M. Bowen. 1988. *Family evaluation: An approach based on Bowen theory*. New York: W.W. Norton.

Kurtz, E. 1979. *Not-God: A history of Alcoholics Anonymous*. Center City, MN: Hazelden.

———. 1993. *The spirituality of imperfection*. New York: Bantam Books.

Larsen, E. 1985. *Stage II recovery: Life beyond addiction*. New York: Harper Collins.

Latner, J. 1973. *The Gestalt therapy book: A holistic guide to the theory, principles and techniques of Gestalt therapy developed by Frederick S. Perls and others*. New York: Bantam Books.

MacLean, P. D. 1978. A mind of three minds: Educating the triune brain. In *Education and the brain: The seventy-seventh yearbook of the National Society for the Study of Education*. Chicago: University of Chicago Press.

Maslow, A. H. 1954. *Motivation and personality*. New York: Harper and Row.

———. 1962. *Toward a psychology of being*. New York: Van Nostrand.

Mooney, R. 2010. Heard quote on an audio recording of one of Bill W.'s presentations, personal communication with author (March 29).

Napier, A. Y., and C. A. Whitaker. 1978. *Family crucible*. New York: Harper and Row.

Perls, F. 1969. *Gestalt therapy verbatim*. Moab, UT: Real People Press.

———. 1973. *The Gestalt approach and eyewitness to therapy*. New York: Bantam Books.

Polster, E. 2005. *A population of selves: A therapeutic exploration of personal diversity*. Gouldsboro, ME: Gestalt Journal Press.

Prather, H. 1970. *Notes to myself*. Moab, UT: Real People Press.

Rogers, C. R. 1961. *On becoming a person: A therapist's view of psychotherapy*. New York: Houghton Mifflin.

Rohr, R. 1992. *The wild man's journey.* Cincinnati, OH: St. Anthony Messenger Press.

Satir, V. 1972. *Peoplemaking.* Palo Alto, CA: Science and Behavioral Books.

Schnarch, D. 1997. *Passionate marriage: Keeping love and intimacy alive in committed relationships.* New York: Henry Holt.

Siegel, D. J. 1999. *The developing mind: How relationships and the brain interact to shape who we are.* New York: Guilford Press.

Tiebout, H. 1999. *The collected writings.* Center City, MN: Hazelden.

Wilson, B. 1957, 1988. The greatest gift of all. In *The language of the heart: Bill W.'s Grapevine writings.* New York: AA Grapevine, 233–36.

———. 1958, 1988. The next frontier: Emotional sobriety. In *The language of the heart: Bill W.'s Grapevine writings.* New York: AA Grapevine, 236–38.

About the Author

Allen Berger, Ph.D., is a nationally recognized expert on the science of recovery. He is the author of Hazelden's popular *12 Stupid Things That Mess Up Recovery*. He is widely recognized for his work in several areas of recovery that include

- integrating modern psychotherapy with the Twelve Steps
- helping new patients understand the benefits of group therapy and how to get the most out of it
- emotional sobriety
- helping families adjust to the challenges of recovery

Dr. Berger is also author of *Love Secrets Revealed,* a book about making relationships work; *How to Get the Most Out of Group Therapy,* a guide for new patients; and *Recovery Matters,* a series of five audio recordings.

Dr. Berger is the clinical director of The Institute for Effective Psychotherapy. He spends his time teaching, speaking, training counselors, and seeing patients and their families in private practice in Southern California. You can learn more about Dr. Berger and his work at www.abphd.com.

Hazelden, a national nonprofit organization founded in 1949, helps people reclaim their lives from the disease of addiction. Built on decades of knowledge and experience, Hazelden offers a comprehensive approach to addiction that addresses the full range of patient, family, and professional needs, including treatment and continuing care for youth and adults, research, higher learning, public education and advocacy, and publishing.

A life of recovery is lived "one day at a time." Hazelden publications, both educational and inspirational, support and strengthen lifelong recovery. In 1954, Hazelden published *Twenty-Four Hours a Day*, the first daily meditation book for recovering alcoholics, and Hazelden continues to publish works to inspire and guide individuals in treatment and recovery, and their loved ones. Professionals who work to prevent and treat addiction also turn to Hazelden for evidence-based curricula, informational materials, and videos for use in schools, treatment programs, and correctional programs.

Through published works, Hazelden extends the reach of hope, encouragement, help, and support to individuals, families, and communities affected by addiction and related issues.

For questions about Hazelden publications, please call **800-328-9000** or visit us online at **hazelden.org/bookstore**.